The adventure began with a speaking date in Germany that led directly to evil's own chambers: Hitler's hotel suite in Berchtesgaden, where DALE EVANS ROGERS played out one of the most extraordinary scenes in her star-studded career.

The celebrated entertainer and bestselling author shares this once-in-a-lifetime trip from the New World to the Old and back again, a highly personal journey from soul-scarred Europe to the Holy Land, where she followed in the steps of Jesus.

Here is a visit you'll never forget, crammed with adventure, insight and revelation. You may have visited the Old World, but you've never truly *seen* it until you travel with Dale Evans Rogers, WHERE HE LEADS.

WHERE
HE
LEADS

Dale Evans Rogers

PILLAR BOOKS NEW YORK

WHERE HE LEADS

A PILLAR BOOK
Published by arrangement with Fleming H. Revell Company

Pillar Books edition published July, 1975

ISBN: 0-515-08021-7

Library of Congress Catalog Card Number: 74-12592

Printed in the United States of America

PILLAR BOOKS is a division of Pyramid Communications, Inc.
919 Third Avenue, New York, New York 10022, U.S.A.

Dear Mom:

*You are now eighty-four years young—yes, <u>young.</u>
As far back as I can remember, you have been
young and beautiful. You give the laugh to today's
"youth syndrome." You have proved to me that
both youth and age are a state of mind. There is
in you a grace and loveliness that has become rich
and richer with the passing years, and before any
more years go flying by, I want to dedicate this
book to you as a bouquet of gratitude—<u>for being
a wonderful mother; for being the great Christian
that you are; for teaching me early about our Lord
Jesus Christ; for never swerving in your faith in
God's promise:</u> "Train up a child in the way he
should go: and when he is old he will not depart
from it"; <u>for being my source of moral and spiritual strength; for helping me to rear and instill in
my son the true values of the Christian life and for
providing the Christian home that led him to
Christ at so early an age; for your witness of trust
in Him in the hard times and crises of my life.</u>*

*You will never know how I have watched you
and gained strength from you when my heart was
breaking.*

Often I have heard you say, "If the Lord has given me any talent at all I don't know what it is —unless it is washing dishes."

Let me say in love that He has given you the most precious gift within His power to give—the talent of being a wonderfully Christian mother— just the greatest!

Your grateful daughter,

Frances

DALE EVANS ROGERS

Contents

Foreword

Travelers are a peculiar breed; some of them travel in sheer curiosity; some to get away from it all; and many of them with preconceived notions and attitudes which color everything they see before they see it.

Dale Evans is surely one of the most traveling celebrities of our time; she is forever "on the go." Recently she went out to Palestine—not in curiosity and not merely to stare—but to find light and strength in following the footsteps of the Master. She went seeking—and she found it!

This book is the record of her seeking and finding in the land called Holy; it is the spiritual log-book of a great religious experience on the road that runs from Bethlehem to Calvary and beyond. She wrote it as a tribute to the mother who started her on that road, and for those of us who dream of some day sitting by the still waters of Galilee and praying at the tomb with the broken door — for those who love this Lord and Land, and for those in need of Him.

And it is more: *This book is her philosophy of life.*

She is quite humble about it all. As her publishers, we are humbled as we read it, glad—and understandably a bit proud—to put such a book in your hands for the living of these days.

FRANK S. MEAD

WHERE HE LEADS

1

Take-Off

The year 1972 was a bad one—crowned with blessing. Hard, nerve-wracking and faith-testing, momentous and painful, it was very much like the song I sing when I go out to witness:

Fill my cup, Lord, fill it up, Lord!

No doubt about it: My cup ran over in '72.

Early in March my mother went into the hospital for surgery—mastectomy (breast surgery). She had already gone through operations for cataracts and a broken hip. I had been with her a year earlier when she was told that she had a malignancy, and what do you think she said?

"Well, I'm not surprised." No hyterics, no tears —just a quiet acceptance of what would come, if God allowed or willed it.

I looked at her and thought of the words of Isaiah: "For the Lord God will help me; therefore shall I not be confounded: therefore have I set my face like a flint . . ." (50:7). Flint is just about the hardest substance you can find.

That's Mom: a flinty Christian.

The doctor thought he had it licked with chemical therapy, but no—now there had to be a second lump. I prayed that this, too, would pass, that this second lump wouldn't be malignant.

With Roy and my brother Hillman, Bill Hansen, our pastor, and my good friend, Judy Atherton, I sat down in the hospital coffee shop to sweat it out. How we prayed that those surgeons might find a benign tumor and not a malignant one! It was an eternity of agony—until one of the surgeons came in, walked over to our table and said, "The tumor is small, but definitely malignant."

The whole place seemed to explode. I leaped to my feet and ran to the hospital chapel with Judy; and we prayed there until the storm passed, and we placed Mom in the hands of the One who had given her life—and faith.

It's almost funny, isn't it, that our first impulse at the announcement of bad news is to run? *Run!* Get away from it. But—run where? Where else but to God? God was waiting for me in that chapel. He sent me back to hear more and better news: the doctor came to tell us that they got all the malignancy without a radical operation. My tears then were tears of joy.

The day after the operation was my brother's

fifty-sixth birthday. We had a little celebration, and he left for Texas that afternoon. I noticed as I watched him walk out to his car that he looked very, very tired—and one of those icy chills ran through my heart. But—no, he'd be all right. . . .

Mom made an amazing recovery. I nursed her through her convalescence, and as she grew stronger, my old routine began again—finishing a book, cross-country witnessing, cutting an album for Word Records. Roy was busy, too. He had slowed down a bit. He wasn't quite well, and the doctors said, "Take it easy." And beyond my concern for Hillman's health, and the usual annoying problems in our business to be faced and solved no matter how sick or tired we were, there was a feeling of nervous exhaustion from my head to my toes. Something told me that I was running out of steam. It was all piling up higher than Pikes Peak, and I wasn't looking forward to the coming summer either. It was packed with personal appearances, fairs and rodeos, and there was to be a public relations tour for my publishers.

All in all, it seemed like just too much, and again I was tempted to run away—to chuck it and forget it.

But again—run where?

We took Mom home to Texas around May 1. She was well enough to travel by then, and my sister-in-law down there wanted to take care of her until she was well enough to go it alone in her own little house. She was in good hands.

Then I remembered.

Some months previous to all this trouble I had received an invitation to speak at a conference (or "retreat") of the Christian women of the U.S. Army at Berchtesgaden in Germany. At first I was tempted to say *no. Me*, flying all the way to Hitler's hangout in the Bavarian Alps? I just wasn't in the mood for it. I began to look for excuses and found plenty of them. I was a female Jonah with more excuses than a centipede has legs. Too busy. All tuckered out. Besides (*à la* Jonah), there was just as much need for me to witness right here at home as there was to go all the way to Germany. Let somebody else go!

But that old persistent voice within kept saying, "*Go!*"

The voice kept telling me, "If those women in Berchtesgaden had faith and spunk enough to stage a retreat right in Hitler's old nest, maybe you should have courage and decency enough to go over there and help them. You'd better go; if you don't, how will you live with yourself?"

Then another idea came: Why only Berchtesgaden? Why stop there? If you go that far, why don't you go where you've wanted to go ever since you dedicated your life to Jesus Christ—to the Holy Land?

I thought Roy might object. Roy said, "*Go.*"

I thought Mom might not like it. Mom said, "*Go.*"

I prayed about it and God said, "*Go.*"

I asked Larry White about it. Larry is pastor of our Chapel in the Canyon in Canoga Park; with his wife, he had conducted many tours in Palestine. Larry said, *"Come on!"* He collected twelve people from the Los Angeles area to join a Gotaas Tour soon flying out of Chicago—forty-seven in all. I could speak at Berchtesgaden on the fifteenth and meet them in Rome on the sixteenth, and go from there (my heart jumped) to Athens, Cairo, Lebanon, and—*Israel!*

It was quite a scramble, but I made it. On May 12 I boarded a Lufthansa plane for the twelve-hour flight to Frankfort. That seemed a long way from home, and the troubles of home were still on my mind. Had I stopped to think it through, I would have remembered that everywhere is home to God—that He is *everywhere.*

If I ascend up into heaven, thou art there. If I make my bed in hell [troubles!] behold, thou art there. If I take the wings of the morning, and dwell in the uttermost parts of the sea; Even there shall thy hand lead me. . . .

Psalms 139:8—10

I was content. I dozed. . . .

2

Germany

I wasn't to doze very long, for in the seat beside me was a young German aerospace engineer from Stuttgart. I couldn't speak a word of German, but he spoke good English, and did we gab! He briefed me on Germany and the German people, and I was more than startled, as we talked, to discover that the German people had a lot in common with the American people. Maybe the World War II bitterness was still too strong in my thinking, but there was nothing bitter in this man's mind.

We talked long into the night. As I left him I thought of the hidden oneness of humanity, the sharing of common hopes, desires, and fears, the mutual seeking for the truth of being and the meaning of life. We agreed that there were good Germans and bad Germans and good Americans and bad Americans. When the conversation got around to religion, I had my chance to witness. I left him with a copy of *Woman at the Well,* autographed to his wife.

Odd, isn't it? I had talked so much about witnessing "right here at home," and here I was witnessing in a plane suspended between the heavens above and the Atlantic below! God leads in mysterious ways.

When we touched down at Amsterdam I got out and started to walk toward the airport building, and almost fell flat on my face. My feet were swollen painfully; I had forgotten to take off my shoes during the long flight. (Remember that, if you ever have to spend long hours in a plane. Your dogs will growl like mad if you don't!)

I walked around the airport understanding nothing anybody was saying, but enjoying the smiles of welcome on the faces of the people. The Dutch are a friendly, lovable, honest people—really honest, as I learned that day. We had twenty minutes in Amsterdam before the plane took off again, and I went roaming happily all over the place snapping pictures with my little Instamatic, and I was so busy that I forgot to watch the clock. I was down on the lower level when the public address system called loading time. I grabbed my purse and ran and I was about to go through the gate when I realized that I had left my camera behind. I jabbered frantically to the gateman, but he didn't understand my Texas-origin English. Finally he said, "Two minutes only."

I raced back—and a girl at the top of the basement stairway called to me and held up my camera. Whatever it was she said, it was a message from the angels. I thanked her in red-faced embarrassment all the way to my seat on the plane. Talk about honesty! What odds would you get on ever seeing that camera again in our beloved U.S.A., where everything has to be nailed down; and you don't dare leave anything unnailed—even in a locked car —in many of our cities!

Believe me, I was impressed by the Hollanders.

It was a short jump to Frankfort, and enjoyable. But as we were about to land, a touch of sadness went through me. Our boy Sandy had died near Frankfort Airport in 1965, while in the army. The tears came but they stopped when Fran Pannell and her husband Bob and their two little girls met me and led me to their car, which was to take us to Heidelberg.

Heidelberg! In the old days Heidelberg was known as an uproarious college town, the seat of a university in which the devil-may-care students mixed duels, songs, and beer parties with their learning. But to be fair, Heidelberg did produce generations of fine scholars. It was a bulwark of the Protestant Reformation. The Heidelberg Catechism, a confession of the Reformed Church, was written here and is still used all over the world. At Heidelberg my religious pilgrimage—and education—had begun.

Everybody was happy in Heidelberg; there was

a festival being observed—The Celebration of the Siege and Burning of the Castle. We saw the ruins of the old castle high on a hill, lighted so that it appeared to be in flames. I mused that some of the fiercest flames of religious conflict had burned in Germany. Luther was a flame, standing there and crying, "Here I stand ... I can do no other!"

Children, parents, and students roamed the streets, arm in arm, looking like the happiest people in the world. It was something to see, as I recalled the devastation of World War II. Joy springs afresh in every generation, doesn't it? There is still hope and faith and laughter. God works out His purpose—one "increasing purpose" as Tennyson put it, in all of us.

It was all very gay and very noisy. I would have appreciated it more if I hadn't been so tired. I crept off to bed at the nearby army base just outside the city and fell asleep thinking of Martin Luther and his flame, of his Reformation—and of my Sandy.

And of Berchtesgaden, tomorrow.

3

"Though he slay me,
yet will I trust in him...."
Job 13:15

Early the next morning, the Pannells collected me
and my baggage and we took off on the wildest
ride of my life. You drive on the Autobahn, from
Frankfort to Berchtesgaden. *Autobahn*, in German, means path for cars—superhighway. It's *super*,
all right! Our Los Angeles Freeway has an awful
reputation for fast driving, but if you think *that's*
fast, just try a German autobahn. They drive like
so many Jehus gone completely wacky, tailgating
at 100 miles an hour, and I'm not exaggerating. No
speed limit! Tiny compact cars whizzed by us as
though we were standing still.

Bob said, "When there's an accident, it's plural
—a terrific pileup of cars." I swear I lost five years'
growth on that road.

But I did get a glimpse, now and then, of the
countryside, which was lovely. Soaring white steeples were everywhere. Bob said they were Catholic
and Lutheran steeples. I thought again of Martin

Luther. What a tremendous courage that man had, waging his desperate battle for reform within the church he loved! He put his life on the line every hour of the day. The persecution he endured was unbelievable—but how it paid off! It was reminiscent of Jesus' fighting the hierarchy of His day, and of the price He paid for speaking out and standing firm, and of the deadly persecutions of the apostles of the early church.

I would have to read up on Martin Luther, when I got home. His fight goes on in us and in our church. It isn't as violent or deadly now as it was in his times, but the lines of division are still being drawn in the Protestantism he inaugurated. We are divided between those who stand like flinty Luther—who are true followers of the Christ—who live unashamed of the gospel and dare to act according to its light—and those who compromise easily and quickly to protect their position and status in our anything-goes society. But it will come out right in the end. I have faith enough to believe that with all my heart. The Bible speaks of the coming "latter days" when there would be a falling away from the faith, of the division of the sheep and the goats, of when the sheep are scattered. Maybe we are in those latter days right now. We sure are scattered, but even the scattering often looks good to me. There are little groups in all the churches meeting in their homes (as the first New Testament Christians met), getting down to the nitty-gritty, to the heart of the matter, enjoying the Christian discipline together, sharing, encouraging, building a new peace and a new church that live within the heart.

I know—we talk about peace, peace, and there seems to be no peace—except the peace of God in the heart of the believer.

"In the world," Jesus told us, "ye shall have tribulation: but be of good cheer; I have overcome the world" (John 16:33).

I thought to myself, as we flew along the autobahn, "Come on, girl. Sure, you've had trouble and tribulation back home, and it almost got you down. But old Job had tribulations far worse than yours, and he had the faith to cry, 'Though he slay me, yet shall I trust him.' And Job made it. Martin Luther had troubles you'll never have, and he made it. So can you."

Lord, forgive my falterings, and lead me to more, more truth.

I say my tribulations had almost put me down. *Almost*—but let me add this: There have been many times in my life when I have beaten my fists against the walls in agony, but since I turned my life over to Jesus Christ, it has never once occurred to me to wail, "Christ, You've let me down." He has *never* let me down. He has always been there to grab my hand and lift me back on my feet again, to strengthen my feeble knees and still the tempests in my heart. Just when the rains and the winds of trouble seemed to have leveled my crop of dreams, I would catch the promise of a fresh root of blessing, and my faith was restored as it was being restored that day in Luther country.

That, my friends, is the name of the game—flinty, durable, living faith.

I can never forget those white steeples. They called out to me, "Look *up*!"

We drove through Munich. We didn't stop, but from the car window I saw enough of it to be fascinated by its cleanliness. The streets were spotless; you could "eat your breakfast on them." Even the centuries-old buildings had a clean dignity about them that caught the eye and the heart. Germany is clean, whatever else you might say about it.

Along the streets, they were putting up poles and flags in expectation of the coming 1972 Olympics. Little did we realize what was to happen in Munich at those games. That *wasn't* clean.

With a shudder, I recalled that it was in Munich that National Socialism—Nazism—was born. Here Adolf Hitler staged his beer-hall *putsch*. He saw half of poor Munich destroyed before he died in his Berlin bunker. And here Cardinal Faulhaber stood like flint against the ghastly corporal from Austria.

Hitler, who knew so little of the saving grace and power of Jesus' blood that he bathed the world in blood.

Hitler!

4

"It had been good for that man if he had not been born."
Matthew 26:24

In the shadows of the late afternoon we climbed the steep winding road to Berchtesgaden, through the quaint little village up to the General Walker Hotel, where I was to speak to six hundred women, Protestant and Catholic. I wondered if such a thing could have happened in Germany under the Nazis. A charming hostess showed me to my quarters and took the wind out of my sails by announcing that this was the suite often occupied by Adolf Hitler! I was about to shout, "No!" when it struck me as being both funny and prophetic. *Me,* here, witnessing for Christ, taking over Hitler's quarters. God had led me here; it would be good.

At dusk I stepped out on the little balcony and looked out over the towering Bavarian Alps. I gasped at the beauty and majesty of it. I murmured, almost subconsciously, "How beautiful

". . . good for that man if he had not been born."
upon the mountains are the feet of him that
bringeth good tidings, that publisheth peace . . ."
(Isaiah 52:7).

I stood there wondering what thoughts must
have gone through the mind of Hitler as he looked
at this triumph of the creating hand of God. Some
of his biographers say he loved it up here—but
was such a mind capable of love? Albert Speer, one
of the Nazi overlords, is probably nearer the truth
when he says in his book, *Inside the Third Reich,*
that Hitler "was more affected by the awesomeness
of the abysses than by the harmony of a landscape."
I can believe that—and I'll bet a bad nickel that he
never looked at those towering mountains and
thought of "good tidings that publisheth peace."

The memory of the man churned through me. I
thought of what he did at the crematories of
Dachau, not far from here; of his fearful genocide;
of his screaming and mesmerizing of crowds of
people, whipping them up to hate, to fight, to win
for what he called the superiority of the Aryan
race. He was the incarnation of evil—a flinty man,
but the flint in him was forged in hell.

Proverbs 14:21 tells us, "There is a way which
seemeth right unto a man, but the end thereof are
the ways of death." I wonder what Hitler thought
of that—if he ever read it. With his wandering,
addled mind, he may have convinced himself that
he was right. He was at first a great hope to his
people—he would lead them to a great future. But
his wicked power grew and his lust for more power

and dominion over the earth ran through him like a cancer until he plunged this beautiful country into ruin and himself into an ignominious death.

Hitler versus Jesus Christ! Hitler lost that one. God wiped him out.

The Hitler suite was comfortable enough but by no means luxurious. The only out-of-the-way thing about it was the bathtub—the longest and widest bathtub I have ever seen.

5

The Sound of Music

We drove over to Salzburg. You breathe music in the air of Salzburg.

Here we saw the home of the von Trapp family —that family of superb musicians whose story is featured in the film *The Sound of Music*. They were a deeply religious family, and if you'll forgive the interruption, I'd like to give you this, about Maria von Trapp, the mother of the brood. It seems that one of her youngsters at breakfast one morning asked her, "Did Jesus have to eat oatmeal for breakfast?" (Bless 'em—the kids are full of questions like that!) I don't know how she answered it, but the question started her on a search to find out what daily life was like in the time of Christ.

"It was," she says, "so heartwarming to discover Jesus—to find out that He was a person. He wasn't a bit like His pictures—those gooey ones, you know, where He looked so goody-goody. They do Him such an injustice that they should be forbidden by the police. If we could only get our dear Lord down from the niches in the churches where we have placed Him, where once a week we go, make our bow, and mentally say, 'Would You kindly stay there?' and go on with life. Christianity of nowadays has turned out to be a Sunday religion with our Lord far, far away, and *very* holy. He will always be very holy, but He can be very close and very much alive. It is one of the most heart-warming findings when you see Jesus right in your home or discover Him as your friend, walking with you through life, holding your hand."

Bless you, Maria. "Lo, I am with you *always* . . ." (Matthew 28:20).

And we saw the home of the great Mozart. As I looked at the personal memoirs, the photographs, and musical scores in his home (now a museum), I thought of what a legacy of music this one man had left the world. Did you know that Mozart got little recognition while he lived—that he was buried in a rainstorm with a handful of people at his grave—and when someone came the next day to put some flowers on his grave not even the attendants in the cemetery knew where he was buried? That happened to him as it happens to many of the great artists among us, but his music remains as some of the best ever written, and now they have an annual Mozart Festival in penitent Salzburg. Too late—and too little!

I doubt that Mozart ever knew how great he was; otherwise, he might never have tried so hard to improve his remarkable talent. He was a man of single mind and purpose: to make more and more beautiful the music God had put in his great heart.

Christians, I think, should be people of single mind and purpose, in that whatever they do should be done for the Lord. The Chistian vocation should encompass every phase of life if it is really to glorify Christ. There is no decision large or small that is unimportant. "In everything give thanks: for this is the will of God in Christ Jesus concerning you" (1 Thessalonians 5:18).

Recently I saw a newspaper picture of a man standing at the door flap of a tent, with the caption, MAN LIVES ALONE FOR 40 YEARS BECAUSE HE'S FED UP WITH THE HUMAN RACE. Now there's a cop-out, if I ever saw one. Who *doesn't* get fed up with the human race and with all the whimperings of men at one time or another? or with the ingratitude of people who don't appreciate you? To become disgusted with men's frailties is one thing, but to run out on humanity is something else. The Bible tells us not to run from it but to stay and cope with it. And even when we are failing to cope, and our overtures to reason together are refused, we can still love people for the sake of Christ—and we can pray! We may not be given the privilege of seeing the fruits of our labors of love, as poor Mozart was never given, but we can depend upon this: The spiritual music of our lives will remain long after we are gone.

I was to hear yet another sound of music in Salzburg—catacombs music. Near the city's catacombs, cut into the bottom of a mountain, there is a chapel two hundred and fifty years old and still in use. Off to the left of this chapel there is a hidden stairway running up to a secret chapel where Christians of another age during dire persecution climbed one thousand steps to reach it.

If you were asked to worship with the police on your heels—would *you* worship? Today would we climb the one thousand steps to worship—with police at our heels?

How flabby is our Christian muscle! We must have air-conditioned churches, with soft cushions on the pews. We are so casual about our Christian freedom to worship when and where and as we please. We have an abundance of Bibles—and yet there are countries in our day and age in which the use of Bibles is frowned upon and even forbidden, and where even a torn scrap of Scripture is denied—and we scarcely are aware of it. Billy Graham has said that we should memorize the Scriptures; hide the Word in our hearts, for the day may come when we will no longer have the Scriptures to read!

The old Salzburgers had to hide themselves with their Bibles; they were God's Underground. "My words," God told them, "shall not pass away" (Matthew 24:35). They shall never pass away—no way, no way—so long as we have such Christians! They kept the faith, kept it alive in their mountain hideaway, in a cave with seats carved out of solid rock on which the baptized members sat while the unbaptized stood through the service. I could hear them singing, and my heart was strangely warmed.

Some of them died and were buried in the catacombs, but even then there was a touch of glory and triumph. We saw plants and living flowers growing in front of the crypts. *Growing* flowers! For the Christian, death is not the end but a phase of an eternally *growing* life. There were flowers, too, in the old cemetery nearby, and at the far end, we found the stone effigy of a German Unknown Soldier. In the days of war he was our enemy; but in his heart he was convinced that he was fighting in a good cause, just as we were convinced of ours. We hated each other in those days; today the hatred is disappearing. All human time, I think, is divided. The writer of Ecclesiastes reminds us that there is "a time to love, and a time to hate; a time of war, and a time of peace" (3:8). It shouldn't be so—but it is.

General Sherman was right: War *is* hell. I accept that judgment; he should know! And yet I have wrestled long with the problem of war, and I have found answers and solutions hard to find. I believe in the duty of defending one's country when it is striving to live as a peaceful nation among the nations of the world. I believe that physical death is not too great a price to pay for a great spiritual or moral ideal, but I want to be sure that this is what we are fighting and dying for.

I believe that war and peace begin in the heart of the individual. I have a favorite song that I love to sing, wherever I go: "Let there be peace on earth, And let it begin with me"—and I mean every word of it because I believe it with all my heart. I believe that we should "If it be possible, as much as lieth in you, live peaceably with all men" (Romans 12:18). But I am sorrowfully aware that there come times in our lives as individuals and as nations when it is impossible to live peaceably with maniacal leaders who in lust and hatred and deceit and aggression turn loose the dogs of war—and I believe that such leaders should be resisted.

I know that Jesus predicted that there would always be wars and rumors of war (see Matthew 24:6)—and I also know that He had a novel way of *preventing* war. He sent His disciples out to teach His love as the solution, unarmed except for the staffs they carried. Love was their only weapon. Peace was in their hearts before they began to preach peace to others. He did not base His Kingdom on armed might. He used force only once: when he drove the money changers from the temple. At best, it seems to me, the only gain in war is a temporary truce—another chance to supplant slaughter with love. When all is said and done, the only peace worth having is the peace of love for God—*and for our neighbor.*

My Sandy died, an American soldier in Germany. This unknown German boy in Salzburg died I know not how. I must love both of them.

We may have to fight in defense, but, dear God, may we learn to hate the aggression and not the aggressor!

That night, back in Berchtesgaden, we had the banquet at which I had come to speak, and once again I was reminded of the oneness of the human race. There were six hundred women in that room, representing a wide variety of backgrounds and religious faith. It was good, and it was stirring; it was a time for witnessing—for all of us. We forgot Hitler and the war, and thought only of Jesus Christ; we sang, and we prayed *together.* All the barriers were down. All the silly little fences of human misunderstanding collapsed, and we were one in the Lord. It was one of my finest hours.

As we walked out into the hotel lobby after the banquet, we heard a radio blare out the news that George Wallace had been shot. It was like a blow in the face. Here I had come all the way from California to Germany to witness to Christ, and while I was doing that a lunatic had tried to kill a presidential candidate in a Maryland super-market! I sat down and tried to keep my cool and to figure out an answer to the gnawing question, "*Why?* Why, dear God, why?"

It was hard for me to accept it—to realize how our country could degenerate to this state of affairs—when a man running for public office is shot for airing his views. We who have condemned the Germans so bitterly for the horrors of Nazism have created a horror of our own that is equally reprehensible. How did we ever sink into this mire of permissiveness in the home, the schools, the church, the courts? Where is the rugged stamina on which this country was built? What is "liberating" about imposing a violent form of so-called government upon a people who want to be free in elections, in the choice of industry, in worship? How did we get this way?

Is not the wrong in *us,* as individuals in whose hearts there really is no desire for the peace and love of God? Aren't we, as old Isaiah said, a people of unclean lips? (*See* Isaiah 6:5.) The all-too-obvious miscarriages of justice, the hypocrisy, the repudiation of marriage, the lust for money, the corruption of power running from Washington to the lowliest crossroads of the land—what a stench! The American eagle flies lower and lower. Is it to die in the ruins of what was once a glory—as died ancient Rome? These questions rolled over and over in my mind as I tried to sleep that night.

Speaking of Rome, we fly there tomorrow.

6

O Rome ... City of the Soul!
Lord Byron

The taxi which took us from the airport didn't just *drive* into Rome; it *dived* into the most terrifying city traffic I have ever seen. It was the autobahn —and worse—for here we were plunging through narrow streets—darting children leaped for their lives from the road to tiny sidewalks—horns honked wildly—every man for himself. You are either quick or you are dead in Roman traffic.

Frightened half to death, I screamed at the driver, "Do you have a lot of accidents over here?"

"Sure we do. But we are more careful than you are in the United States, because there are no speed limits. One thing sure: when we have a wreck, it's a beauty. No cripples left." That shut me up like a clam. For once in her life this Texan had no answer—just dumb amazement. I hung onto my hat and closed my eyes and hoped we'd make it to the hotel. We made it; I thanked St. Christopher, or whichever saint it is in charge of automobiles.

We forgot the noise and panic of the streets when we walked into the Sistine Chapel at St. Peter's. It was so beautiful that it hurt. The walls and ceiling of this room are covered with murals painted by the incomparable Michelangelo. They tell the whole story of man from his Creation and Fall and punishment and Redemption, to the Last Judgment. One man did this, in one lifetime.

I remember especially the picture in which he shows God reaching out to touch the finger of an inert human Adam. Adam is lying down; he looks lazy and only half-interested—a man, but not yet a "living soul." But the figure of the Creator is quite different: God *strains* to touch Adam's finger, straining so hard to close that awful gap. All the energy is in God, not in apathetic Adam. We can rejoice that God touched His man and closed the gap—for us.

In the painting of the Last Judgment, the old artist got in a bit of righteous humor. Here a dour-faced man in ecclesiastical robes stands guiding a group of lost souls toward a flaming, smoking furnace. Our guide said, "Look at the face on that man. It is the face of a pesky bishop who was constantly plaguing Michelangelo to hurry up and get his work done." Good for Michel!

In the Basilica of St. Peter is the *Pietà*, that magnificent sculptured figure of Mary holding her crucified Son in her arms. Her face is the face of a young girl. (Said the artist, "The Virgin never grows old.") If tears do not sting your eyes when you see the *Pietà*, there's something wrong with your soul.

Two days after we were there, a demented man mutilated the *Pietà*, knocking off an arm and one eye from the figure of Mary. How sad, to mutilate the memory of the mother of Jesus Christ!

Forgive us, Father, for mutilating her memory—and His—every day, in our hearts!

There is "soul" in the *Pietà;* there is soul in the ecstatic marble effigy of St. Cecelia the Martyr, whose hands are said to be the most beautiful and lifelike hands ever carved by any sculptor. There is soul, too, in every mile of the catacombs of Rome, filled with the tombs of other martyrs. The catacombs are dark and dank—*frightening* when we think of the uncounted number of Christians buried there—*glorious* as we realize that these Christians *worshiped* there. Caught worshiping, they could be thrown to the lions in the Roman circus or burned to death as human torches in the gardens of Nero. *But they worshiped.*

Everyone who goes to Rome goes to see the Colosseum and the Circus Maximus. I stood in the middle of that old Colosseum and looked up at the tiers of circular seats which once held forty-five thousand Romans. They screamed their thirst for murder at the gladiators fighting for their lives in the sand where I was standing. We are told that some Christians were thrown to the lions in the Colosseum, but there were probably very few. The lions were used not here but in the Circus Maximus, just down the road, in the horrendous "lion games" in which the half-starved beasts were let loose on Christians confined in cages. How many died such terrible deaths we will never know, but it is said that those martyrs marched through the streets on their way to death at the Circus with radiant faces and singing their faith songs; and that unbelievers along the way were known to join them in death.

We modern Christians say it's hard to be a Christian today. What do we mean, *hard?* Compared with what these Roman martyrs suffered, we have it pretty easy!

I had two reactions to the Colosseum and the Circus. At the Circus, I visualized those cages in the arena and I thought of those P.O.W.'s in Viet Nam, in *their* cages. More than one of them said, "I never could have made it if it hadn't been for the Presence of Jesus Christ with me in that prison!" It was the same Christ—in old Rome and in Indochina. This Christ is as alive and as powerful as ever.

In the Colosseum I visualized the gladiatorial games and the bloody contests staged there for the amusement of a bloodthirsty mob. I thanked God that we had come a long way from all that—and then I got to wondering whether we had come far enough! We still seem to relish ferocity in some of our so-called sports. In the boxing ring crowds cheer the blow that cuts an eye or smashes an opponent's nose; in football we cheer the vicious tackle. But for the grace of God and the influence of Christianity and the thin veneer of civilization, we'd be as bad as those old Romans. The old savage lurks in all of us. Consider the morbid interest in the automobile crash, or watch people grab the newspaper with the most lurid details of the latest murder!

Still, it *is* better since Christ came, isn't it? With Him we saw a new Spirit in man, or available to man, and a new reverence for human life. I think God led me to Rome's Colosseum and Circus to better understand just that—to the city in which Paul was beheaded and Peter crucified—and I was lifted up and strengthened.

I was to meet Paul again in Athens.

7

"Ye men of Athens, I perceive...."
Acts 17:22

Athens was named for Athena, goddess of youth and peace and war and wisdom. She was also patroness of the arts and crafts and guardian of the cities in the misty, mythological days of Greek mystery religion. *There* was a liberated woman—in CAPITALS! Legend tells us that she competed with Poseidon (Neptune) for the dominion of Greece. Neptune struck his spear into a rock and salt water poured out; Athena struck the same rock and an olive tree shot up. Hence the name of the city: Athens. Twelve thousand slaves built for her a temple that still makes architects gasp: the Parthenon. In it they put a statue of the goddess carved of ivory and gold. Blessed be Athena of the Athenians!

This Parthenon is Exhibit *A* on the hill called the Acropolis. In Greek, Acropolis meant "high point of the city"; it was an area devoted to philosophic and religious purposes. But when the converted, wandering Jew named Paul came to town, he preached an immortal sermon in which he hinted that their high hill wasn't enough, and that their religion wasn't enough, either. Paul was well aware—as we are aware—that the Greeks had made a real contribution to the onward and upward march of man. They gave the world a whole line of superb scholars and philosophers, and even Christianity finds itself in debt to Plato and Platonism. Good—but not good enough, said the man of Tarsus: "Ye men of Athens, I perceive that in all things ye are too *superstitious."*

Bull's eye, Paul! It was superstition—and worse. Even their beautiful Parthenon was "the virgin's place," and from Mars Hill, where he preached his sermon, he could see the Porch of the Virgins where worship to the Virgin Athena was performed with the aid of sexual relations with the temple prostitutes. This was religion? Not for Paul. Not for me. I gagged at the thought and then hung my head as I remembered the sex orgies we were tolerating back home—the rotten films, the lewd bars, the widespread pornography. I looked at the ruins of Greece as I had looked at the ruins of Rome and saw the disaster of a people obsessed with themselves, with their pride of intellect and their physical lust, and I thought of my own land.

There was music in the streets of Athens, fountains splashing, floodlighted ruins all around us.

We walked those streets at night completely without fear. Women walked it alone with no male to protect them from muggers or murderers—something we hesitate to do in many an American city. I couldn't understand how this was possible in Athens until I was reminded that Greece lives under a military dictatorship in which crime in the streets simply isn't tolerated. (Must we have a dictatorship, to get that?)

My nephew, who obtained leave from his U.S. Air Force post there, took me to the Flea Market where we ate spiced lamb, tomatoes, and green peppers, all rolled up in a pancake. I paid for that —later. The first rule of tourism is, "Be careful what you eat in a strange country." This, I believe, was the beginning of stomach trouble for me.

We climbed Mars Hill and sat down where Paul had preached, and one of the ministers in the party took out his New Testament and read the sermon. May I give it to you, as the new Living Bible gives it to us?

Men of Athens, I notice that you are very religious, for as I was out walking I saw your many altars, and one of them had this inscription on it—"To the Unknown God." You have been worshipping him without knowing who he is, and now I want to tell you about him.

He made the world and everything in it, and since he is Lord of heaven and earth, he doesn't live in man-made temples; and human

hands can't minister to his needs—for he has
no needs! He himself gives life and breath to
everything, and satisfies every need there is.
He created all the people of the world from
one man, Adam, and scattered the nations
across the face of the earth. He decided before-
hand which should rise and fall, and when.
He determined their boundaries.

His purpose in all of this is that they should
seek after God, and perhaps feel their way
toward him and find him—though he is not
far from any of us. For in him we live and
move and are! As one of your own poets says
it, "We are the sons of God." If this is true,
we shouldn't think of God as an idol made by
men from gold or silver or chipped from stone.
God tolerated man's past ignorance about
these things, but now he commands everyone
to put away idols and worship only him. For
he has set a day for justly judging the world
by the man he has appointed, and has pointed
him out by bringing him back to life again.

Acts 17:22-31 LB

Some of the intellectuals in the crowd broke into
laughter at this mention of the Resurrection, but
some others "wanted to hear more about this
later." They heard more. A lot more. In the sixth
century their beautiful temple, Parthenon, became
a Christian church! Their gold-and-ivory statue
(idol) of Athena became a relic of a dead past.

Paul spoke on Mars Hill because they wouldn't let him speak anywhere else. In Athens, a non-Greek was permitted to speak to a Greek only across Mars Hill, and as a non-Greek he was forbidden to speak to a citizen in their precious Parthenon, or anywhere else on the Acropolis. He spoke, and shattered the myths of that temple and philosophy: "He hath made all men of one blood" (*see* Acts 17:26).

Sure, they laughed him out of Athens, and that hurt Paul more than anything else had ever hurt him. He "departed from Athens, and came to Corinth" (18:1). So did we. He walked or rode a donkey; we rode a bus. We rode comfortably through the rolling hills around Corinth (it reminded me so of California), and we walked dutifully through more ruins.

They looked quite like the other ruins we had seen (see one, see all!). But riding out of Corinth, the old stones spoke to me of what this city had meant to Paul. He loved the city and the people—and that took a lot of loving. Corinth was the largest and most cosmopolitan city in Greece. Venus was worshiped by most of the people, and the very name of the place was another word for *immorality,* and some of the Christians accepted that. Paul laid down the law to them. He condemned their moral weaknesses, the "party spirit" in their church, their sexual promiscuity, and their lackadaisical lightheartedness about marriage and public worship. He even criticized them for eating meat that had been offered to pagan idols. I can just hear them complaining about his interference in their private lives. He was *meddling,* and they didn't like that. (It all reminds me of the old mountaineer down South who enjoyed a visiting preacher's sermon up to the point where the parson said something about moonshining, and then he shouted, "Now you've stopped preachin' and begun to meddle!")

Paul meddled because he loved them, even though they didn't love him.

Forgive us, Lord, for our resentment of Christian rebuke—for closing our ears to what we should hear from You but do not want to hear!

Paul said to the Corinthians, "Now abideth faith, hope, charity, these three; but the greatest of these is charity" (1 Corinthians 13:13). I remember that about Corinth. I have already forgotten the ruins.

8

"Woe to them that go down to Egypt...."
Isaiah 31:1

On the plane from Athens to Cairo we talked expectantly of the land of Egypt, of Moses and Joseph, of the Infant Jesus in Mary's arms, of the great pharaohs who built the pyramids and the sphinx and the tombs filled with treasure. Egypt should be good.

We found it a country filled with mixed wonders and woe. The woe met us at the airport at 2:30 (A.M., Ma'am). We had looked forward to something of a welcome, but what we got was a chill of hostility on the faces of a crowd looking down on us from a balcony. It made us shudder, and wonder what it meant. Later we were told that we were the first foreign visitors allowed into Cairo since the imposition of a ban against tourists thirty days before. They'd had a lot of trouble with foreigners in Egypt; you've read about it. We were advised not to mention that we were going from there into Israel, but simply to say that our next stop was Lebanon—which was the truth but hardly the whole truth. We walked a tightrope in Egypt.

At the hotel an attendant brought a bottle of water to my room. He looked me up and down with knowing eyebrows. He made me vaguely uncomfortable. I had the same experience with another fresh one who "helped" me off the camel I rode up to the pyramids. I felt like slapping him, or even going further than that.

I discovered that woman's place in Egypt isn't what it is in the United States—by a long shot.

Their attitude toward women over there is encouraged, alas, by many western women who are out looking for kicks, and who laugh at the insults. They offer real encouragement to the men-on-the-prowl in Egypt who have come to believe that any woman traveling without an escort is fair game. It's as much our fault as it is theirs, and I didn't like any of it.

But there are wonders galore in Egypt. The pyramids—tombs that date back to 5000 B.C., resplendent with paintings and sculpture—the huge statues of the pharaohs—are really something. I was quite impressed by the number of statues erected in memory of the great Rameses II, who is supposed to have given Egypt her great golden age of splendor and power (with the help of a multitude of slaves!). Rameses had an idea that the Egyptians could dam up the Nile for irrigation purposes and stop the too-frequent famines that swept the land, but he never got around to it. He had 700 wives and 300 concubines and he just didn't have time.

Their Mohammed Ali Mosque in Cairo was impressive. I watched the Moslem worshipers wash their feet *five times* before they entered it to pray, and it made me think of man's natural desire to stand clean in the presence of God; of the Pharisees criticizing the disciples for eating with unwashed hands; and of Jesus' sharp retort to them in which He suggested that the washing of the lips and heart was more important than the washing of the hands; and of Lady Macbeth trying to wash the blood of murder from her hands, moaning, "Out, damned spot!" when the water failed to wash it off, nor would "all the perfumes of Arabia . . . sweeten this little hand."

We must respect the Moslem's desire to cleanse himself. Even more, I believe, we must respect the Christian teaching of the cleansing of the soul by the sacrificed blood of Jesus Christ. We can wash and wash and wash the body, but the stain of sin remains until we are convinced that ". . . without the shedding of [His] blood, there is no remission [of sin]" (Hebrews 9:22). I *know* it is the only way, for it has happened to me.

Egypt is a happy hunting ground for the archaeologist and the antiquarian. I respect them for digging up the monuments and cities and temples and truths of the past, but to be honest about it,

I am much more interested in the religion of the future.

R. Earl Allen, in his book *Bible Comparisons,* has a little story about one of the Ptolemy line of Egyptian kings who built a huge lighthouse. He commissioned an architect named Sostratus to design it, and instructed him to make it worthy of the great Ptolemy, whose name was to be inscribed upon its surface so that all men might see it. Sostratus, who didn't see why the king should have *all* the credit, inscribed his own name on the stone walls, covered it with a thick layer of plaster, and put the king's name on the plaster. Time and the wind and the waves wore the plaster away, and the name SOSTRATUS was left standing out in bold relief.

I like that. It reminds me that even the names of the kings and the pharaohs and the great generals and statesmen, will, in time, be obliterated —and the name of God will stand out in bold relief —the God under the plaster—the God behind and in all things—the everlasting God.

As we left Egypt we passed the tomb of Gamal Abdal Nasser, guarded by soldiers who stood at their post around the clock. It is decorated perpetually with fresh flowers and near it we saw a "flame tree" which seemed to be afire. To me it looked like a Royal Poinciana tree, and it was symbolic of the smoldering fire that threatens Egypt now. I was glad to get away from the threat of its heat.

9

No Cedars in Lebanon

Beirut in Lebanon is a gem of a city, full of tradition and history and battles. It's where St. George is said to have killed the ancient dragon, if you're interested in dragons (which I'm not). Beirut was interesting to me because it is the romantic gateway to Palestine, and I couldn't wait to go through that gate.

I made one bad mistake in Beirut: I began drinking unbottled water in the hotel dining room, and I drank it as though water was going out of style, plus partaking of too much fruit. (Lebanon is called "The Fruit Basket of the Middle East" and the fruit is luscious—too luscious!)

I didn't see enough of Beirut to write anything about it. We took off too soon on a bus jaunt along the Lebanon coast to Sidon and Tyre. The minute we got in the bus, I told the driver that whatever happened, I wanted to see the famous cedars of Lebanon, and he said okay. I trusted him; he promised to let me know when we came to the cedars. I waited and I waited and I waited. No cedars. Maybe we took the wrong road. No cedars at all!

Jesus visited both Sidon and Tyre. When we saw the gleaming rooftops of Tyre in the distance I recalled the Scripture: ". . . he arose, and went into the borders of Tyre and Sidon . . . [and] a certain woman, whose young daughter had an unclean spirit . . . came and fell at his feet" (Mark 7:24, 25). The woman of Sidon! Her sick child! This was the first of a series of experiences I was to have in the Holy Land. I identified with her; I felt her pain, her anxiety—and I sensed that as Christ had led her to peace, He had led *me*. There were centuries between that woman and me, but the thrill, the healing, was the same. Closer than a brother, closer than hands and feet He was to her and to me. I could almost see her, in Sidon.

Tyre was the city of King Hiram who, according to our guide, was the granddaddy of Freemasonry. He helped Solomon build the famous temple in Jerusalem. He cut down the best cedars he could find in Lebanon and shipped them over sea and land to Jerusalem. ("Any cedars yet, driver?" "Nope.") Maybe Hiram was the reason I wasn't seeing any cedars; maybe he helped himself too generously! I had just about given up when the driver said, "There's one!" *One!* I got a glimpse of it through the window, and then even that one was forever lost. It could have been a eucalyptus or an oak. I wouldn't know. Oh, well . . . .

I was restless in Tyre and Sidon, for I knew that Upper Galilee was "just over the hill." A real hill flashed into sight—Mount Hermon. It is as old as the early psalmist who sang, "Tabor and Hermon shall rejoice in thy name" (Psalms 89:12). Jesus was there. Tradition calls it The Mount of the Transfiguration. I looked up at its majestic summit through misty eyes.

They say you can see the whole of the Holy Land from the top of Hermon—from Lebanon and Damascus and Tyre through the mountains of Upper Galilee and all down the long winding course of the Jordan from the Sea of Galilee to the Dead Sea. I longed to see that, but we didn't have time. We did stop for lunch in a little restaurant at the foot of Hermon in the center of great fields of wheat and barley. The houses were built of what looked like cement or stone with grapevines on their roofs for insulation. It takes five years for a vine to cover a roof. There were also acres of trees busy producing bananas that tasted like the bananas of Hawaii.

I ate too much and drank too much of that unbottled water.

I wanted to stay there in the shadow of Hermon and just absorb it all, and talk awhile with the Transfigured One. Some day I'll go back and do just that. But it wasn't to be on this trip; we had to get back to the hotel. On the way back we stopped at Baalbek, to see the best-preserved ruins of the old Roman Empire. I was getting a bit fed up with ruins by this time, and I didn't exactly relish the idea of another set—until I saw what they had in Baalbek.

Baalbek is a community of colossal temples of Jupiter, Bacchus (Dionysus), Venus, and Mercury. Their foundation stones are enormous—30 by 13 by 10 feet; three stones in the enclosure walls are each 64 feet long, 14 feet high and 15 feet wide, and each of these blocks weighs about 1500 tons. From them, great granite columns rise high, high, high toward the cloudless blue sky above. Archaeologists tell us that much of this stone was imported from Egypt, but how they got them there from Egypt nobody knows. Nor do we know how they ever got such gigantic and heavy stones up so high. Modern architects look at it and shake their heads. The guides have one explanation: "There was always the sword." Thousands of slaves built it, and many of them died there.

Legends run like wildfire at Baalbek: it is said that Adam died near here, that here Cain built his first town as a refuge; that Noah lies buried somewhere nearby; that Abraham lived here for awhile; that Solomon built here a temple to Baal as a gift to his concubines and then double-crossed the concubines and gave it to the Queen of Sheba. Maybe so, maybe not. Maybe Jesus came to Baalbek, maybe not.

All that's left of it is the whisper of a dead grandeur. The whisper is haunting, but the ruins are symbolic of the fall of the religions of Rome. Constantine ordered the destruction of these temples; some few were saved and converted into Christian churches. The civilization that created it offered a brief challenge to Christianity, and Christianity accepted the challenge—and won. says Dr. Norman Vincent Peale of Baalbek in his book *Adventures in the Holy Land:*

So, too, may the culture of our own modern era—in so many ways identifiable with the sophistication of these ancient times—be penetrated spiritually. Christianity has proved its ability to identify and be at home in any age and for all people.

On the way back to Beirut, my stomach was rumbling like Vesuvius.

10

"And... departing from the coasts
of Tyre and Sidon, he came unto
the sea of Galilee...."
Mark 7:31

I slept the sleep of the just that night, dreaming
that with the dawn I'd be starting for Galilee.
Whittier has a line that goes

> As on the Sea of Galilee
> The Christ is whispering, "Peace."

There would be peace there, where I would begin
walking in His steps.

It was a good dream, and a good idea, but it
didn't work out that way at all. As I started to
pack, I broke out in a cold sweat and fell back on
the bed. I rang for a strong cup of tea, gulped it
down, and somehow made it aboard the bus and
to the airport. I couldn't even go through customs;
my friend Myra White did it for me. Nausea, dizzi-

ness, and dysentery. What a day! All I could pray was, "Lord, behold thy miserable servant."

I give you a real gem of wisdom, ye would-be tourists: BE CAREFUL WHAT YOU EAT AND DRINK WHEN YOU TRAVEL, LEST THE SKY FALL ON YOUR ACHING HEAD. (You'd better believe it!)

It was a long hard drive to Safad, just above the Sea of Galilee. At times I wanted to die; the next second I wanted to live. It was a misery relieved in part by an excellent guide named Max. Max was a Levite Jew, and I learned a lot from him. Did that man know the Bible! The Old *and* New Testaments jumped alive as we made our way north. As we rolled into Safad he told us that this was the city Jesus referred to when he spoke of "a city that is set on a hill cannot be hid" (Matthew 5:14). Please don't think me irreverent, but most of it remained "hid" from me. I staggered to bed—and stayed there.

Max found a doctor for me who prescribed pills, tea, and matzo. And more matzo. Matzo is unleavened bread (in the form of large crackers) eaten by the Jews at Passovertime. It was all I could hold on my aching stomach, and I ate all I could hold. I pitied the poor Jews who ate this matzo while they were stumbling through the Old Testament wilderness. They ate it because they were in a hurry, and couldn't wait for their bread to rise. In time, it became a staple of the Jewish diet. I had a lot of sympathy for them as we started across Galilee,

and I knew what our Lord meant when He said
that "man cannot live by bread alone."

Paul speaks of ". . . the unleavened bread of
sincerity and truth" (1 Corinthians 5:8), which
explains a little of the kind of bread that Jesus was
talking about. The good matzo kept me alive and
helped me back on my feet, but the Holy Spirit
helped more. Without the Spirit's help I could
never have made that trip. All that day, alternately
praising the Lord and rebuking Satan, I managed
to enjoy everything as I felt strength flowing slowly
back into my heart and body.

We stopped at the Mount of Beatitudes, where
Jesus is believed to have preached His Sermon on
the Mount (*see* Matthew 5:7). It really isn't a
mountain, but a saddle-shaped hill called The
Horns of Hattin. Biblical scholars and writers have
not yet been able to solve the question as to when
and how a hill becomes a so-called mount. In most
cases the mount is a special place where something
special happened, and so *mount* seems more impressive and appropriate than just *hill*.

Be it hill or mount, it sang to me, and I forgot
that I had ever been ill or worried. I *heard* Him
say, "Blessed are the poor in spirit"—that was for
me. "Blessed are they that mourn"; the mourning
of past years dropped from me like a shabby, out-
worn cloak as He comforted *me*. "Blessed are they
which do hunger and thirst after righteousness";
He had filled my life with riches beyond reckon-
ing, and I prayed for the strength to always be

hungry and thirsty for more of His truth. These words of His Sermon on the Mount rang out like the chimes of a cathedral bell. It is holy ground—still. One must spiritually take off his shoes as he stands there.

Clinging to a slope at the northern tip of this Sea of Galilee is Bethsaida, and close by Bethsaida was the place where Jesus fed the five thousand. It was Andrew, "a local boy," who came to Jesus that day and said, "There is a lad here, which hath five barley loaves, and two small fishes . . ." (John 6:9). And He fed them. I used to wonder about that miracle when I was young and full of doubts—but no more, since He has fed me. Stop wondering! Isn't it enough to know that we can never get beyond His love and care?

And there's another thing to remember about this day of feeding: Jesus fed them with the help of a boy's hand. A hand like yours and mine. *Use my hand, Lord. . . .*

> Take my hands, and let them move
> At the impulse of thy love.

Use me and lead *me, Master, lest someone die of hunger!*

On another occasion Jesus condemned Bethsaida, and Chorazin, and—Capernaum, which was "exalted to heaven, but would be cast down in hell" (*see* Luke 10:15).

We went down the road to Capernaum.

Cast down? Capernaum sure looks cast down today; you wander in heaps of rubble. But I was exalted there. There were memories that blessed Jesus preached here in the headquarters town of His Galilean ministry. He talked about taxes, and He told the disciples to pay their taxes and to render unto Caesar whatever belonged to Caesar and to God what was rightfully God's. There are lovely oleanders partially hiding the rubble, and an old olive press, and at the heart of it stands a reconstruction of the synagogue in which He preached and taught. Instinctively, one closes his eyes in Capernaum, and is taught, and led.

Max told us that in the days of Jesus and long after His departure, the women of the town sat in the balcony of that synagogue, and the men on the main floor. Male chauvinism! There was no electronic loud-speaker system, of course, and often, when the women couldn't hear what was being said by the speakers, they would lean over the balcony and call out to their menfolk and ask what was going on. Max told us that this was why Paul told the women to keep silent in the churches (*see* 1 Corinthians 14:34). It could be. It was good for me to hear about those women, for I do quite a lot of witnessing in the churches, and Paul's statement has bothered me (a little, but not too much!) Max also told us that every synagogue in the land was built facing Jerusalem.

There is a little steamer at Capernaum that

takes tourists for a ride on "deep, blue Galilee."
We got aboard, and I settled down for a little rest
in a comfortable chair. But it wasn't to be. I was
asked to sing "The Man from Galilee" to the crowd
gathered on deck—without accompaniment. I didn't
want to sing; my throat felt as out of shape as my
stomach, but I couldn't refuse. If the Lord would
help me, I'd do it.

Put your hand in the hand of the man who
stilled the waters . . . .

I stood there and looked out over the shimmering
waters of Galilee and thought of the thrill the
disciples must have had in this same spot, with the
Master aboard, when the storm that came up so
suddenly nearly capsized their boat. Galilee can be
as smooth as a millpond one moment and the next
moment a gale will come ripping out of one of
those little canyons along the shore, and your boat
tosses like a cork. Instant tempest. Jesus said to
those disciples in their little tempest-tossed boat,
"Why are ye fearful, O ye of little faith?" (*see*
Matthew 8:26). (Why are you fearful, Dale Evans?
Sing!)

I sang, I think, as I had never sung before or
since in all my life. Never have I experienced such
joy in singing any other song. For me He walked
over there on the shore. He asked, "[Children,]
have ye here any meat . . . ?" (Luke 24:41).

The sea of life can seem smooth and eternally

peaceful at times, and then our voyage is interrupted by an unexpectedly vicious storm. The wise will make sure that the Galilean is aboard both in the stillness and the storm.

We lunched at a kibbutz—one of those collective agricultural communities that have attracted so much attention all over the world. They are really worth attention in *any* country. When a would-be farmer comes to Israel without the cash to start farming on his own, he goes to a kibbutz where he works cooperatively with others in the same boat, or goes to school and learns a trade. He can stay there as long as he wants to stay, provided he keeps up his allotted piece of land or works at his trade. If he gets lazy and goofs off, out he goes. No welfare problem here. Everybody works, *and everyboy likes it.* The food is excellent, the buildings are solid and attractive and well built. The grounds around them are well kept, and the people are just out of this world. You've never seen enthusiasm until you've seen a kibbutz. Everybody sings and everybody shares in the profits of their work. They have a tremendous faith in the future—which is also something in this day and age!

Then came Nazareth.

Cradled in the Galilean hills lies Nazareth, the immortal little town that has meant so much to so many. From the tops of those hills you can see the gleaming summits of Mount Carmel to the west, Hermon to the north, the hills and valleys of Gilead to the east. Running in those hills, the young Jesus developed the far look. He was not to be limited to the boundaries of the town from which, it was said, nothing good could come. (*See* John 1:46, "Can any good thing come out of Nazareth?")

Today Nazareth has forty thousand people—60 percent Moslem, 40 percent Christian (Catholic). According to Josephus, the first Christians there were called Nazarenes. That would be about A.D. 35-90.

Over the cave, which is said to have been the home of Mary and Joseph, there has been built the Church of the Annunciation—a good name—inasmuch as it was here that the angel announced to Mary that she would be the mother of Jesus. Behind Mary's Cave is the Grotto of the Holy Family, including the carpenter shop. It is a beautiful church, containing some precious mosaics, but somehow, as one sees it, one wishes that it might have been built somewhere nearby instead of right on the spot. If the site had been left in its original form, it might be easier for us to catch those angelic words: "... Blessed art thou among women ..." (Luke 1:28).

I might have thought more of the blessedness of women if it hadn't been for a man and a woman and a donkey I met in the streets of Nazareth. They were Arabs, and the man rode the donkey and the woman *walked*. Worse still, the woman was carrying a child; still worse, she was lugging a huge bundle on her other arm. The man sat up there

like the king of all creation, totally oblivious of
the burdens borne by his wife. It made me stinging
mad—something one should never be, in Nazareth!
—but I snapped a picture of them, and when it
was developed later, the man's head was lopped
off. I had a good laugh and I wasn't a bit sorry.

Our guide explained to us that this man-rides-
while-the-woman-walks idea is accepted as a way of
life in Arab communities. Women are inferior
beings to the Arabian male. An Arabian woman is
not permitted to leave her house without her husband or an escort of her husband's approval—with
one exception: she can go out alone only to fetch
water from the community well and carry it home
on her head. If she goes out alone and without per-
mission, especially at night, the guide told us, the
husband can kill her! This is considered justifiable
homicide, for the poor woman has "dishonored"
the man of the house.

I was indelibly impressed by the spectacle of that
woman walking while the man rode the donkey.
I still can't get her out of my mind, especially when
I hear some Women's Lib advocate sounding off
about how we western women are slaves and sex
objects and all that, and—if you'll excuse the interruption—I'd like to get something off my chest
about that!

It took this trip to the Middle East to make me
see how lucky and free we western females really
are, and to wonder why there is such a howl about
our so-called liberation. I wonder why we feel such

a need to be liberated—from *what*, and to *what?* What's behind all that? Is it pride, or is it an honest desire to function more freely in a vocation to which God has called us? If it is pride, there can be no real satisfaction in the enlargement of our present opportunities for women. But if it is truly a desire to be of greater service to God, then I believe it is worth fighting for. However, I wonder if that is the whole picture.

I always enjoy talking to women's groups and discussing this question with them, for I believe that what women think and do (especially in the art of raising their children) will have a powerful influence upon the future as it has in the past. It is said that behind every good and successful man there is the influence of a good woman who has recognized her true identity and purpose as a woman, deemed it a gift from God, and used her talents, abilities, sympathies, and understandings to strengthen and support the man she loves, whether as mother, wife, sister, or whatever. I am not opposed to the true liberation of women which was begun two thousand years ago in the teachings of the Christ. Before He came women were chattels; they voiced no opinions; they married at the whims of their fathers. Let a woman be caught in adultery and she could be stoned to death (why wasn't the *man* stoned with her?). When Jesus set free the woman taken in adultery, the uplift of woman to a higher estate really began.

Modern American mothers cut their hair or let

it grow long, vote for presidents, go out and get themselves jobs, do pretty much as they please with their time, their money, and their children. Any mother in Israel, under the Roman occupation of Jesus' time, would have been punished severely for even dreaming of doing anything like that. Men held her in contempt; she was her man's property. Divorce under Rome was a way of life. Seneca, in the days of the apostles, spoke of daily divorces and says that Maecenas was married a thousand (!) times. Saint Jerome tells of a woman who had been married twenty-three times and the Samaritan woman with whom Jesus talked had at least five husbands. Even Reno might envy those records, but Reno is accepted as a national scandal while Rome accepted it as a matter of course.

Man is man and woman is woman, Women's Lib notwithstanding. At one time, I would have been a rousing, fighting woman's libber, for the man of my first marriage had broken my heart. I decided then and there that, forced to get a divorce, I would be a success in the world, do things my own way, make a place for my son and myself. The divorce had set me free to do just that.

But many years later came the *true* liberation; I gave my life to Christ and I was liberated in the Spirit. ". . . where the Spirit of the Lord is, there is liberty" (2 Corinthians 3:17). So I believe in "lib"—provided we get the values straight.

'Tis no small thing to be a woman. I have found no greater joy than that of holding your child in your arms, of being a loving partner to your man, of being childbearer and the keeper of the fires of home. Great mothers, great women friends, and helpers are the leavening in the great unwieldy lump of today's society.

I thought in Nazareth of the dear mother I had left back home. She is a great part of the leavening of my life. She is one of those women who, according to Women's Lib, has held a "second-rate job" as wife, mother, and friend. I see red when I hear such women condemned for holding that position and that job. I think this second-rate job calls for more on the ball than any other job in the world. I speak from experience. I have worked on both sides of the fence.

Let us, as mothers, train up our children in the way they should go. Let us grant the father his rightful place in the home. Together, let us ask the Heavenly Father to lead us in wisdom and love to a better future. If there is any other job more worthwhile and necessary, I haven't heard of it yet.

Well! Forgive me for this long dissertation inspired by that Nazareth woman stumbling along beside her lofty man on his donkey. I *had* to get it off my chest.

11

"Then cometh he to a city of Samaria, which is called Sychar...."
John 4:5

Driving out of Nazareth we saw two old battle-grounds. One was called The Mount of Precipitation—the place where the angry people of the town tried to throw Jesus over a cliff after he had preached in their synagogue. I thought of His courage as He faced them, and I wondered what I would have done if I had been in that mob. It's hard for us to understand why anyone would want to throw the Man of Nazareth over a cliff—but we weren't there. I pondered what I would have done, and thought about it. Would I have scoffed at Him and rebelled at His meddling in my life? I honestly don't know. The same battle of rebellion against His Way still goes on in our hearts, where we crucify Him daily. Or do we crucify ourselves?

We sped across the line that separates Galilee from Samaria. We had to cross Samaria to get to

Jerusalem. Like Jesus, we "must needs go through
Samaria" (John 4:4). My heart began to pound;
there was something I had to see in Samaria above
all else I might see over here.

Max pointed out a second battlefield along the
way: the Plain of Megiddo. Some of the world's
most decisive battles had been fought on this low,
fertile plain. Alexander the Great took a licking
there; its soil was stained red with the blood of
Egyptians, Canaanites, and Assyrians. Joshua killed
a pagan king there; Napoleon suffered one of his
few defeats, and Allenby crossed it on his way to
Jerusalem.

We saw it covered with farmers' fields. A man
was ploughing down there. It looked quite peaceful—now.

Max announced, "Look—over there—that is Sy-
char. We shall be at Jacob's Well in a few minutes." I almost shouted, "Stop the bus; I want to
get off!" I wanted to run, but no . . . I almost
trembled as I walked to that old well dug by father
Jacob, so long ago. You who have read my book
Woman at the Well will know why. I had based
that book on a woman at that well.

We are told that when a man is drowning, his
whole life story races through his mind. Through
my mind now raced the story of Jesus sitting by
this well and talking with a sad and lonely Samaritan woman despised by both her own people *and*
the Jews, who hated all Samaritans. Few Jews ever
ventured into Samaria—but Jesus did. To His fel-

low Jews it was like putting His head in a noose, but He *had* to go there! He had something to say to the Samaritans.

He arrived at the well in the heat of the day, exhausted, thirsty, hungry. He rested here, while His disciples went off searching for food. Perhaps he sat thinking of Jacob, or of princely Joseph, whose grave was nearby, or of Joshua and Gideon and the early kings of Israel who came there to drink. Whatever His thoughts, the soliloquy was broken by the appearance of a Samaritan woman. Any other rabbi would have either run from her or driven her away.

He did neither; He said to her, "[Woman,] Give me to drink" (John 4:7).

"Sir, thou hast nothing to draw with" (v. 11)— no rope on which to let down a bucket. She was thinking of common water in a desert well, but as they talked she began to understand that He was talking of *living* water that comes up out of the heart to quench all thirst forever and to give everlasting life.

Ah, you woman at the well! Even now, centuries later, I know your mind and heart, for once I had come thirsting to my Lord for the uncommon waters of the Spirit, and my thirst was satisfied for the first time and for all time, and my poor blundering life changed forever. As my own son had led me to Him, this Christ had led me here to commune with you in understanding and in love.

Woman of Samaria! You had come here that day

alone, at noon, when the other women of your village would not be there. They looked upon you as one looks upon a leper, with their eyes, if not their lips screaming, "Unclean! Unclean!" You came to the well unclean; you left it cleansed.

It had happened to me, too; she and I were one.

Off in the distance, as she and Jesus talked, they could see Mount Gerizim. Before 300 B.C., the Samaritans had built a temple there in which to worship *their* true God. Down in Jerusalem the Jews had built a temple in which to worship *their* true God. "Our [Samaritan] fathers," said the woman, "worshipped in this mountain; and ye say, that in Jerusalem is the place where men ought to worship" (v. 20). Which was the right place? That's the old quarrel—which of us worships correctly the correct God in the correct place? The old gesture of difference, conflict, intolerance! In which mountain, Lord? In neither and in both, He replied. The time would come—the time *had* come when He came—when every man and woman would worship the true God in spirit and in truth *in every place.* (*See* vs. 23, 24). In Gerizim, Jerusalem, Europe, California, Timbuktu. Wherever the Lord is there shall we worship—there shall we find Him.

Dear Lord, why haven't we had the sense to take that story and those words to heart? Why are we still bogged down in racial and religious suspicion and dispute quite as bad as that of the Jews and the Samaritans? Why haven't we the sense and the courage to simply sit down with Jesus and talk it out? He has the answers. When she said wistfully that all things would be made clear when the all-knowing Messiah came, He said to her, "I that speak unto thee am he" (v. 26).

Jesus has come; He is here. He speaks to the Samaritan in every one of us. Lord, open our eyes and ears, that we may see and hear and accept.

I dropped a stone down Jacob's Well and waited to hear it splash so far below. I drank a cup of its cool waters; the act seemed a sacrament. We walked slowly back to the bus, and I turned for one last look as we drove away. I knew what President Kennedy meant when he stood in front of Robert E. Lee's home in Arlington, Virginia, looked toward Washington and said, "I wish I could stay here forever."

The countryside slipped by, like a setting for a play on a stage. It was good to behold. There were endless rows of trees, planted in the early spring—pine, sycamore, eucalyptus, cedar, acacia. Teams of Israeli youth had planted them and would watch over them for eighteen months until they could stand on their own. Max said that the people of Israel felt compelled to make the land look as it had looked in Solomon's time, to fulfill the prophecy of Isaiah 35:1:

> The wilderness and the solitary place shall be
> glad for them; and the desert shall rejoice, and
> blossom as the rose.

This land *has* blossomed; this barren soil has been reclaimed. Even the choking desert around the Dead Sea has taken on new life under these tireless and inspired Israelis. And it is *clean*.

How wonderful it would be if we Americans showed such pride and spirit in our land. How great, if we had the same compulsion in the matter of ecology! Our minister at home tells of one family near Apple Valley that gives one day a week to picking up papers and trash along our roadsides. Can you imagine what our United States would look like if enough of us got the same idea?

We were jarred back into modern times as we drove past Golan Heights, a battlefield of The Six-Day War with Egypt and later the "Yom Kippur War" of 1973. Israel claims that she got the strategy for winning The Six-Day War "right out of the Old Testament." I learned something about that war that I had not known before: what really sparked it was the action of the Arabs in trying to cut off the water that flowed in Jordan, harming the desert potential. That did it. We could still see Israeli fortifications along the hills and the roads. The country was still mined. We shuddered, and walked close to our guide.

Shiloh flashed by—Shiloh—the first holy place in Israel, where the temple containing the Ark of the Covenant was built. The people of Shiloh became wicked and God allowed the Ark to be taken to Jerusalem.

Jerusalem lay just ahead of us.

12

"O Jerusalem, Jerusalem, thou that killest the prophets...."
Matthew 23:37

We came into Jerusalem at sundown, and it was both delightful and depressing. Delightful because of all this city has meant on the history of our faith. In the earliest times it was called Urushalem which traditionally meant "City of Peace," but city of peace is wasn't. It was a city built and destroyed and rebuilt and destroyed I know not how many times, and it might easily be called "The City of the Setting Sun." Many a prophet was killed here. Jesus spent the last days and hours of His life within these walls. H. V. Morton says that when Jesus saw it in the days of Herod Antipas it looked like "a lion crouched in the sun, watchful, vindictive, and ready to kill." So you can see why it was also depressing.

Yet hope springs eternal in Jerusalem for not one religion but three: Moslems, Christians, and Jews come to Jerusalem by thousands and tens of thousands every year, to pray and to sing their hope. It is the religious capital of the world.

It is a city of woe, war, worship, and wailing.

We went out that very night to visit the Wailing Wall. We walked through the little narrow, winding streets (*so* narrow!), past rows of shuttered shops that would become Bedlam and Babel in the morning, and came upon the Wall at the edge of the temple area. There were not many there, that night, but there were a few of the faithful touching it reverently and murmuring their prayers. This is Israel's national shrine of prayer, where supplication is continually made for the restoration of Zion's glory. Maybe I shouldn't have done it, but I reached out and touched it and said a prayer for a Jewish friend back in Palm Springs.

It was an awesome experience there in the night silence, with the stars shining brightly in the sky overhead, and centuries of history calling down to us from the old, old walls. We were quiet as we walked back to our bus through the moonlit streets.

I wanted to see everything in Jerusalem. *Everything.* But I knew I couldn't do that; you can spend a month in this city and not see it all. I'd have to settle on what I wanted most to see.

Come along with me, now, and let Him lead us from the temple to Calvary and the tomb and the Resurrection.

Let's go up to the temple area and sit for awhile in the warm, eternal sunshine on one of the steps, or at the foot of an old column, and see with Him the city He loved and over which He wept in frustrated love. We will find it a city not so much to be seen as to be heard.

Over there on the edge of the area is the Dome of the Rock—now a Moslem mosque and called the most beautiful building in the Moslem world. The ground on which it stands is the ground on which King David stood talking with Araunah about buying a piece of his land, for this was "the threshingplace of Araunah the Jebusite." (Read the story in 2 Samuel 24.) On that pinnacle of rock Araunah separated his wheat from the chaff; on this rock (the Moslems say) Abraham held a knife over Isaac; on it once stood Mohammed; on it Solomon built an altar of sacrifice before his great temple. For the Christian, it marks the site of the temple of Herod the Great, which was under construction when the boy Jesus sat and talked with and confounded the most learned scholars of Jerusalem.

Jesus was twelve years old when He sat there, and He saw that temple often between twelve and thirty. He probably came every Passover to pray there. During one Passover He drove a gang of profiteering money changers from the sacred courts of the temple: "My house shall be called the house of prayer; but ye have made it a den of thieves" (Matthew 21:13). (Have you noticed that these words are followed with "And the blind and the lame came to him in the temple; and he healed them"?)

Lord, what have I done to Your temple in my heart?

Somewhere near where we sat He stood and cried, "If any man thirst, let him come unto me and drink" (John 7:37). Some who heard Him say that said, "This is the Christ" (v. 41). Some rough and tough officers of the chief priest and the Pharisees, commissioned to arrest Him, were afraid to arrest Him and *they* said, "Never man spake like this man" (v. 46). Over there a woman taken in adultery lay crouching on the ground, waiting for the first deadly stone. Jesus told her to go and sin no more, and she walked off down the crowded streets with the power to sin no more.

He has put such power within the reach of all of us!

We saw the Moslems going into the Mosque of the Rock to pray; we saw how they stopped at the door and washed their feet *five times* before entering, leaving their shoes or sandals outside. "Put off thy shoes from off thy feet: for the place whereon thou standest is holy ground" (Exodus 3:5; Acts 7:33). We do not do this, as Christians, yet it is inherent in us to stand clean in the Presence of God.

How blessedly merciful our God has been to provide the blood of His Son to cleanse us from all sin! How sad that so many miss this great deliverance—and what a responsibility we who have experienced it have to tell it to the world. I thanked the Arabs for their Fountain of Purification at the mosque's door.

On Mount Zion we went over to the building where we found what is held to be the Upper Room in which Jesus had His Last Supper. We were disappointed—no, *ashamed*—for in a lower room there is a frightful museum containing relics of the sufferings of the Jews under Hitler. Soap made from the fat of Jews cremated in Nazi ovens, lamp shades made of their skin. It was too much, and we were glad to leave the place.

Then we went out through the eastern gate down the Kidron Valley and up the slope of the Mount of Olives. Along the way we passed many whitewashed tombstones. ("Woe unto you . . . for ye are like unto whited sepulchres . . ." Matthew 23:27.) And we came to a lovely church in a lovely garden called Gethsemane. It is small (perhaps half an acre, for a modern highway has cut the original garden in two) with only a few old olive trees hidden from sight by a high stone wall. We cannot get into the Garden of Gethsemane itself; it is forbidden to enter there, thanks to thoughtless tourists who have trampled on the grass and flowers and torn leaves from the trees for souvenirs.

Why is it that a few ruin it for so many who would walk in reverence there?

We can look through the trees of Gethsemane and see the Golden Gate of Jerusalem—sealed up now, only to be opened on the day of His return to earth. It was through this gate that He entered Jerusalem on Palm Sunday.

But the church of All Nations, at the Garden site, is worth our whole trip to Palestine. An architectural gem, it was built with contributions made by many nations, and it sheltered the Rock of Agony, the bitter rock where Jesus prayed in His loneliness, "O my Father, if it be possible, let this cup pass from me . . ." (Matthew 26:39).

(As I stood there with tears racing down my cheeks, I thought of the painting of the Crucifixion at Forest Lawn Cemetery in Glendale, California, where our three children—Robin, Sandy, and Debbie—are at rest. Jesus is pictured standing with upraised face, resigned to the will of the Father as the soldiers prepare the Cross for Him, with the shouting crowd surging and pushing—and a few "sorrowing." So it is. The crowds desert the fallen hero. Only those who love Him remain when He goes down. With the Lord, this process is reversed: He is closest to us when *we* are down, for, being a Man acquainted with grief, He understands.)

I, too, Lord, have become acquainted with grief. I, too, have had my rocks of agony, but when I surrender my will, for me it passes—like a black cloud passing to reveal the stars.

Gethsemane made us weep; so did the Via Dolorosa, the Way of Sorrows in the city along which He bore His cross. The present Via, of course, is not the original one, but it is as meaningful. Pilgrims come every year to follow Him to the Church of the Holy Sepulchre, which, it is claimed, is built over the sites of Calvary and Joseph of Arimathea's tomb.

This church is a great sprawling, dark, dank structure smoke-filled from incense. There are almost constant processions and services being held by the Greek Orthodox, Roman Catholic, Armenian, Jacobite, Syrian, and Coptic priests and monks who hold a monopoly on the place. No others are allowed to publicly worship here. Each group guards almost desperately its own specially assigned territory within the church itself and riots have broken out more than once. (Two were killed when a Greek swept one more step on a stairway than he was supposed to sweep!) There is endless parading, singing and chanting and ringing of bells.

We were shown the stone on which the body of Jesus was anointed for burial; it was put there in 1808. And we saw the column to which He was bound and scourged, which was first mentioned as a relic in 1384. We viewed the spot supposed to be Calvary, discovered by Constantine's mother, Helena, and identified by her as the true Calvary, and the tomb from which He came on Easter morning. Some say Helena's Calvary is authentic; some say it isn't. I don't know, and I doubt that anyone really knows.

If you plan to go to the Holy Land, a word of caution may help you. Many of the so-called holy places inside the walls of Jerusalem are to be questioned, for the simple reason that Jerusalem has been destroyed and rebuilt so many times. Those who rebuilt didn't bother to clear away the rubbish, but built their new city right on the ruins of the old. In some places, the present street level is sixty feet above that of the original city, and the streets of the Old City average at least twenty feet above the level of the same streets in the days of Christ.

No, you are not walking the very same streets He walked in Jerusalem, but you are very close to it—as close as one can get today. I think a good rule for the Christian tourist to follow would be this: in Jerusalem there is doubt about many so-called sacred spots, but once you get out beyond the walls of Jerusalem, you are *really* walking where He walked. The hillsides of Galilee and Judea haven't changed since He was there.

For instance, there is the Garden Tomb, or Gordon's Calvary, which lies very close to Jerusalem's walls, but still beyond them. Many Christian scholars and researchers believe this to be the authentic site of the Crucifixion and the tomb in which Christ was buried.

There's a good little story about this. The site is named for General Charles George "Chinese" Gordon, the British hero of the Taiping Rebellion in China who died later at Khartoum, Africa. Gordon was sitting one day on a Jerusalem rooftop, looking out over the surrounding hills north of the Damascus Gate, and all of a sudden he saw one hill that looked exactly like a skull. Two caves in the side of the hill formed the eyes, a projection of rock formed a perfect nose, and a larger opening formed the mouth. The top was round, like the top of a skull, and Gordon realized that *this* might be the "Place of a Skull"—the true biblical Calvary which lay beyond the walls where Jesus was actually crucified. It became even more probable when a tomb was found beneath the hill.

I shall never forget, as long as I live, the hours I spent there. As we walked down from the lovely garden to the tomb, I saw it as I had always pictured it in my mind. We formed a line and stepped inside the rock-hewn doorway. There was a young girl kneeling there, isolated in prayer with her lips pronouncing words of prayer from a small black-bound book. She never raised her eyes to look at us. An attendant said she had been there sitting on that cold stone floor all afternoon. Each of us said a silent prayer for her as we walked out, and then held a communion service of our own in the garden overlooking the tomb. It was the most meaningful sacrament of my life.

There is a minister at the tomb, a Hollander named John Van Der Hooven. He served the elements of the Supper and preached a beautiful and brilliant little sermon on the Resurrection. He invited us to attend a service in the garden the following Sunday, and we accepted almost before the words were out of his mouth. Larry White asked him if it would be possible for me to sing at this service. He hesitated; he'd probably had such requests from every party that visited the place.

Larry, nonplussed for a moment, said, "This is Dale Evans Rogers. I know you've heard of her."

No, he hadn't heard of her.

"She is the wife of Roy Rogers, the cowboy. I know you've heard of him."

No. Sorry. He'd never heard of Roy Rogers.

Poor Larry made one last desperate attempt: "She wrote a book called *Angel Unaware*. Have you heard . . . ?"

A smile flashed across his face. "Oh! *Angel Unaware?* Yes, yes. Of course she will sing at the service."

He told me then that we had much in common. His brother had been born Mongoloid, like our Robin, and the book had meant much to his whole family. I was introduced to Dr. Van Der Hooven's parents and their retarded son, a young man in his twenties. I learned that the father had also written a little book about this boy; he called it *Slant-Eyed Angel!*

How many whom we shall never know share our heartaches! How good it is to know that we can help them.

The next Sunday morning I stood in what to me is the holiest place in the world and sang "In the Garden." That was the first song I had ever sung in public—at the age of nine. I thought then that it was the finest hymn in the book, but being only nine I couldn't quite understand how anyone could "walk and talk with Him." This time, I knew. How I ever controlled my voice I'll never know. I had no accompaniment except that of the warbling of the birds flying around us and the rustle of leaves in the soft breeze—and the knowledge that He had led me here to sing.

I thought, as I sang, of my mother, who had heard me sing the same song in the little Baptist Church in Osceolo, Arkansas—and of how she would have enjoyed being there at the tomb with me—and of Robin and that slant-eyed angel of Dr. Van Der Hooven. Mother had once said to me, "There is no hurt like that of losing a child," and I had said, "Mom, we never lose our loved ones in the risen Christ. He promised that what happened to Him could happen to us, and believing that, the hurt passes." I knew how true that was, now that I stood singing for Him at the very doorway in the tomb from which He had come.

My little Dodie, when she was very young, said she wanted to *see* God, to *touch* Him. I felt His hand on my shoulder, that day.

13

"...in thy dark streets shineth the everlasting light...."

Have you read the little poem by William R. Stidger, about Bethlehem?

> Judean hills are holy,
> Judean hills are fair,
> For one can find the footprints
> Of Jesus, everywhere.

We glided through these holy hills beyond grim Jerusalem, out to the place where He was born. He ran on these country hilltops, He dreamed here as He never could have dreamed in a brawling, crowded, filthy city.

The first sight of Bethlehem, of its domes and minarets against the sky, bring ecstasy. Madeleine Miller describes it as lying "Sunned white and sweet on olived slopes, God-lighted with Judah's hopes." No wonder Phillips Brooks thought of it as a place in which were met the hopes and fears of all the years. A tiny place—the hub of history!

It is a town indeed silent in comparison with Jerusalem. Dr. H. V. Morton says it is a little town of white houses which "cluster on the hill like a group of startled nuns." I love that. Nuns indeed are there; they appear on the streets, together with housewives, in gowns and veils and high head-dresses which is a throwback to the days of the Crusades. From the shops of merchants and crafts-men come smiling greetings. I paused in the street to snap a picture of an Arab child and mother. She glanced up, saw the camera, and ran with her child into their house. To them the camera was "the evil eye," which would bring them bad luck.

Down this very street Joseph led his donkey and knocked on the door of the famous—or infamous—inn in which there was no room.

There is a church—The Church of the Nativity—built by Constantine and Helena where the inn once stood. You enter this church through a low and very narrow door—so low that a midget would have to stoop to get through it. It was built that way to keep out wandering dogs, sheep, and infi-dels, and to let only Christians in. One has to bow his head low as he approaches the birthplace of Jesus Christ. Appropriate!

The nave of the church is exquisite, from the ancient mosaics in the floor to the tops of great shining red stone columns. It has three gleaming altars belonging to the Greek Orthodox and the Armenians. You turn from them and walk down a narrow flight of rocky stairs, and there it is—the room in which He was born. This is the stable—not a stable like our western barns, but a cave carved out of solid rock—a hole in the ground.

It is a small place, perhaps 40 feet by 12, with walls 10 feet high; sixteen lamps of gold and silver burn there day and night; and set in the floor is a silver star surrounded by an inscription which reads, *"Hic de Virgine Maria Jesus Christus natus est"* (HERE JESUS CHRIST WAS BORN OF THE VIRGIN MARY). We stand in silence; prayer comes as naturally as breathing. Here it all began. Here God split human history in two—B.C. and A.D., and gave His Light in the form of a Babe.

Lower, there were other caves, one dedicated to the memory of the innocents slain by Herod; another in which St. Jerome labored more than thirty years to give us a new version of the Bible as he translated it from Aramaic into Greek and Latin —our precious Vulgate.

We went back up the winding stairs and out through the little low door and into the blessed Judean sunshine and went off down the road past Shepherd's Field and the Field of Boaz. It seemed like a dream. That five miles of road between Jerusalem and Bethlehem is God's glory road—the King's Highway!

I had come a long, long way to see Bethlehem, but it took on a meaning for me that it had never

had before I came. I know now what Madeleine
Miller means when she writes:

> It isn't far to Bethlehem Town!
> It's anywhere that Christ comes down
> And finds in people's friendly face
> A welcome and abiding place.
> The road to Bethlehem runs right through
> The homes of folks like me and you.

14

Death on the Rock

On our last day in Palestine we drove down to the Dead Sea country and the Rock of Masada. You really do drive *down;* geographically, this is the lowest place on earth. It really *looks* dead. Talk about hell on earth! Here it is! Set in the Negeb (or Negev) Desert, it has all of two inches of rain a year, a maximum humidity of 12 percent. The thermometer read 128 degrees the day we were there. Stepping off the bus was like walking into the fiery furnace of Nebuchadnezzar. (Abednego, here we come!) The Dead Sea is well named—yet it contains high percentages of sulphur, potash, and bitumen, and the Israelis are making good use of that.

The great rock called Masada rises out of the floor of this desert; its name means *stronghold,* and for a very good reason it has become a national shrine of Israel. It has always been a place of refuge. It was a fortress used by the Maccabees when they were fighting the Greeks, and some say that Saul and David hid themselves up there.

When Herod the Great arrived on the scene, he improved its fortifications against the two enemies he feared most: the Romans and the Egyptians. He also made it a playground, complete with a great palace and a sauna bath; he piped up water from the Jordon and ran it over heated rock cylinders which turned the water into steam. Our guide said with a sly grin that it was Herod's San Clemente. (Wonder what he meant by that?)

Its top is 820 feet above the desert; it measures about 20 acres and the only way to get up there (Herod planned it well!) is by way of a steep and narrow path called the Serpent. Any besieging army trying to capture it had to come up that path.

The Roman army came under Titus in A.D. 70, after the fall of Jerusalem; they took all the towns and cities surrounding Masada and with eleven thousand Roman soldiers and twelve thousand slaves drew a strangling circle from which there was no escape. Titus had them like jackrabbits at a roundup. He started pounding at the rock, and kept it up for three long years. The Jews were well stocked with food and supplies; they had plenty of arrows, boiling oil, and stones to hurl at the besiegers. But—three years!

Incredibly, the Romans climbed the Serpent path and built a ramp to the top, ran out batter-

ing rams and catapults and slowly pounded the
fortress to pieces. Down at the foot of the rock a
famous Jew named Josephus (and a Roman citizen) called up to them to surrender and save themselves, but he might as well have been shouting
into the desert wind. The Jews had no intention of
surrendering. Eleazar, their commander, had convinced them that death was better than surrender.

What those Jews did is beyond comprehension.
First, the soldiers killed their wives and children;
then they slew the garrison, all but ten men. Then
the ten picked one man to kill the other nine, and
this last one searched the whole area to make sure
there would be no survivors. He set fire to what
was left of Herod's palace and fell on his own
sword.

When the Romans came over the ramp in the
morning they found 960 dead bodies—and two live
women and five children who had hidden in an
underground pipe.

No, all this has nothing to do with Jesus Christ
(who was baptized not far from here near Jericho)
except that possibly it bore out His statement that
those who take the sword perish by the sword.
What a perishing it was. What a courage these
Jews had, atop Masada. What a people they have
been and still are—dispersed—driven—massacred—
but with the indomitable courage throwing the
torch of their faith to a surviving remnant who
kept it alive! Differ with them as we may, we are
compelled to admire their undaunted spirit.

Neither Roman nor Greek at Masada had yet realized that Christ's way of peace and love was stronger than the sword.

But for that matter, have we?

15

The Show Goes On

We flew out of Israel on Monday, May 29; we went through customs at the Lod airport at 8 A.M. The next night, at 10:30 P.M., a group of pilgrims from Puerto Rico was slaughtered by Arab terrorists as they went through the same customs line. Senseless—horrible. I do not know why we were spared, but God knows, and I leave it there.

By the time we reached Kennedy Airport in New York, I was a walking zombie. Twenty-eight and a half hours in a plane, without a change of clothing! Physically, I was exhausted. I wondered how I could ever pick up the old routine of work again.

We in the entertainment business have a pet slogan: THE SHOW MUST GO ON. Sometimes I think we carry that to ridiculous limits, but spiritually it has great meaning to me. *Life* must go on, come joy or sorrow, failure or success. A man dies—and at the same moment—a baby is born. We can never know what will happen to any of us between birth and death. Things happen that only God can explain, but for me, since this walk with Him in Palestine, I am content to know that He knows what He is doing when He gives a baby life or takes a loved one from us. *His* show goes on, come what may. I will play my part in it as He leads me to play it.

Literally, *our* show began again—the fairs and the rodeos and the personal appearances—and before I knew it I was back in the old routine. I had to fly down to Texas to help Mom dispose of her home and enter the convalescent home where she would spend the fair-and-rodeo months. Then she spends the winters with me in California. Have you ever had to do a job like that? Believe me, it's rough.

My brother and I were discussing plans for the future, one night, when he threw himself across Mom's bed and fell asleep almost instantly. He had been complaining of being tired, during the recent months, but on that bed he looked completely exhausted. We couldn't talk him into seeing a doctor; he was too busy. He was fifty-six years old.

Roy and I were in Nashville for a recording session at the end of August. We were in the studio, and Roy was singing his "Cowboy's Prayer" when a girl from the office came into the control room and handed me a note. It read, DALE EVANS: CALL ITALY, TEXAS. URGENT. My heart went down like an express elevator. This would be Mom, either in trouble, or . . . ! I ran for a phone, put through the call, and heard an almost lifeless voice from the other end. It was Bennie, Hillman's wife. She said, "Well, Frances, Hillman's gone."

"*Gone?* What do you mean?"

"Dead, Frances. A heart attack in his hotel room in New York this morning. He died before they could get him to the hospital."

It was worse than shock; I almost fainted—and then the face of my mother came clear before me. Hillman had meant so much to her. He was her baby, and he had almost died in infancy. She leaned on him for his advice in everything. He was the one who could always cheer her out of any gloom. He was one of those people who can just walk into a room and brighten it.

I asked Bennie to go to her and stay with her until I could get there. The next hour was undiluted agony. I hardly knew what I was doing or saying. We still *had* to record two songs that day. I sang but I'll never know how. I was a numbed machine muttering words, but somehow I got through it. The show must go on.

We had a lot of trouble making arrangements to ship my brother's body by air to Texas. He had died "out of state," and the red tape was infuriating. I was frantic with the delay, until our manager, Art Rush, took over and cleared it. In an hour and a half we were on the plane. Blessed Art! What a rock!

Mom held her head high and stood straight in all her five-feet-plus-a-tiny-bit through the funeral. I held her shoulder so tight during the service at the church that I'm sure she had a bruise. It was difficult but sweet companionship in sorrow. We both missed him—terribly. He was very special to both of us. I could communicate with him. We knew things about each other, the shortcomings, the stumblings, the good things. We were very close. I loved him devotedly, and delighted in his success in business and for his record in the air force in Okinawa and Hawaii. He had an inborn integrity which people sensed instinctively—and trusted. It was inconceivable to me that he could be gone.

How could "the show" possibly go on without him?

We had all fretted, at times, because he wasn't as regular in church attendance as we wished, and one day I blurted out to him, "Are you all right with the Lord?"

He looked me straight in the eye and said, "Sis, don't worry about me; I'm all right with the Lord." That was good enough for me. I knew how many unselfish things he had done for others, but he was never one to toot his own horn. The record was enough. He believed in doing—not in saying. He accepted Christ and he belonged to the church, and that was good. It was better when he said, "I am all right with the Lord." When he said that, my heart knew peace about him.

Of course, there were difficult days after it was all over. Those who die often have the easiest part. It's the going on living that's hard for those who are left. There were times when I felt alone—so alone—without him. Try as I would, I couldn't erase that picture of my brother in his casket. Spiritually, I knew better, but the flesh was bugging me.

In tears one night I started to pray, beseeching the Lord for some sign that would sweep away the loneliness. This was the third time in my Christian experience of nearly twenty-five years that I had turned to Him in utter desolation, and I asked for a tangible sign that all was well. I prayed and I waited, hoping, hoping—and suddenly I felt a gentle pressure on my whole body, as though invisible hands were soothing me in assurance that God was in that room. My mind cleared. I knew then, surely, that the spirit of my beloved brother had returned to the God who gave it, and I thanked Him, breathed a deep sigh of relief—and slept long past the dawn.

In the morning, the shadows were gone and I felt as the disciples must have felt the morning after they found Him walking, risen, on those shores in Galilee. This is God's Way. Don't fight it. *Let Him lead.*

Prayer! I couldn't live without it; I would have died a dozen times if it had not been for my chance to talk it over with God, and gain strength in it from Him.

Maybe this will give you an idea of what I think prayer is, and what it has done for me.

While Roy was in the hospital with an angina

flare-up during Christmas, 1972, I was asked to speak in Los Angeles at a kick-off luncheon of Christian leaders for KEY '73. I took the letters from *PRAYER,* and prayerfully considered them in definitive terms for myself.

P—*Prayer* to me means *praise* to our Lord for His daily benefits, for His unerring guidance in the blueprints of our lives—which He alone understands—since the Bible says, "For of him, and through him, and to him, are all things" (Romans 11:36). Prayer means *petition* for the things we need, according to His will. The Bible says if a son asks his father for bread, will he give him a stone? And if he asks for a fish, will he give him a serpent? (*see* Matthew 7:9, 10). If we give things to our children, then certainly our Heavenly Father will give us the good gifts. Prayer means *pardon* for our waywardness, our failures, if you will—our sins of omission and commission. The Bible says, "He is faithful and just to forgive us our sins, and to cleanse us from all unrighteousness" (1 John 1:9).

R—*R* stands for *renewal.* The psalmist prays, "Create in me a clean heart, O God: and renew a right spirit within me" (Psalms 51:10). *R* stands for *resting* in Him, knowing that we can depend upon the Scripture, "Be still, and know that I am God" (Psalms 46-10). He will not fail us. *R* stands for the *realization* of His Presence in our lives at all times. *R* stands for *repentance,* and for *righting* the wrong in our lives.

A—*A* stands for *adoration* of our God, for *acknowledging* Him in all our ways and knowing that He will direct our paths.

Y—*Y* stands for *yes* to God when our heart cries *no!* *Y* stands for *yield* not to temptation, but resist the devil and he will flee from you (*see* James 4:7). *Y* stands for the *yoke* of our Lord, which is easy, and which He said to take upon us— and to know that because of Him, our burdens are light (*see* Matthew 11:29, 30).

E—*E* stands for *emancipation* from slavery to self— when we yield to the Lord, finding freedom for our souls. *E* stands for *emancipation* from the petty worries and trials of life while we consciously go to prayer and fellowship with the Lord.

R—*R* stands for *ready* at all times to meet the Lord. In other words, to be "prayed up." *R* stands for *reading* His Word daily. *R* stands for *redemption* through the Cross of our Lord. *R* stands for *reaping* what we sow—whether good or bad. *R* stands for *remedy* for our sin—the blood of Jesus Christ, shed for this purpose. *R* stands for *renouncing* those things of which our heart convicts us as being sinful for us personally. *R* stands for *reaching up* in dire circumstances, instead of leaning on our own understanding.

16

"I, Mindy, Take Thee, Jon...."

Back and forth, now, flew the shuttle of our lives, weaving alternately trouble and joy, as it must. New unexpected shadows came, and in God's time flew away, and bursts of happiness took their place.

Roy's doctor found Roy's blood pressure was much too high. He was put in intensive care for a week, and then moved up to a room in St. Mary's Hospital in Apple Valley where we celebrated our twenty-fifth wedding anniversary. We hadn't expected that, and I know of a few other places in which I would like to have celebrated this occasion. But as it worked out, I think we had a better time—just the two of us—in that little hospital over those two little trays of food. That is just the point: We were *together*, after all the pains and pleasures of a quarter of a century. It was a day made for us to be glad; we made the most of it—and it was a day to remember.

My Mom was happy in her Texas convalescent home. After two cataract operations she could see, and after all her other troubles and illnesses, she was getting about remarkably well for a woman of eighty-four, visiting the others in the home, helping those who needed help, and happy at being needed. We all need to be needed, and to be loved. That's what it's all about, isn't it?

Funny thing happened. In one motel, as I checked in, the receptionist gave me the wrong key, and I walked blithely into a man's occupied room. Getting off a plane on another trip, one of those big bumbling fellows said to me (*loudly*), "So you're Dale Evans! Well, I used to watch you when I was nothin' but a kid. That makes us both pretty old, doesn't it?" (Accompanied by an uproarious guffaw.)

Maybe I should have ignored it but I'm not built that way. I shouted back at him: "You may be old, mister, but I'm not. I'm never going to get old. To me, age is a state of mind!"

The crowd laughed, but really, it's no joke to me. I believe it because my Christ has told me that those who believe in Him shall never die (*see* John 3:36), and that following Him through the years gives us life more and more abundant (*see* v. 10:10). This old house of flesh that I live in is slowly weakening and will crumble, but its tenant looks forward *now* to moving into a better mansion in a better place. He that believeth on the Son hath everlasting life. There is no such thing as old age in eternity—and I'm living in eternity *now*.

Another day I flew down to Middlesboro, Kentucky, to sing and witness at a crusade conducted by Dr. E. J. Daniels. Old Boy Satan followed me down there, with his bag full of tricks. Everything went wrong. There was a huge crowd in the big tent—and no fans—and a humidity that smothered you. An overflow crowd sat or stood outside. When I sat down at the piano, the microphone went dead. Then the heavens opened and the rain came down in sheets, and most of the crowd outside just jumped up and ran for their lives.

After the service Dr. Daniels said, "Well, Dale, the devil sure pulled out all the stops to ruin us tonight, didn't he? But he didn't. We had a good meeting, and we'll have a good crusade." Sure enough, he did.

Even in the planes, as I flew hither and yon all over the country, I heard the Good News. Pilots came to tell me of their faith; stewardesses came to tell me of their walks with Christ and of His Presence with them on every flight. They have a Christian Fellowship of Air Line Personnel that is working miracles. I love them and I think it's high time they got a better press than they get in some of the smutty books that are being written about them.

Then came Mindy's wedding.

We had been invited to attend the wedding of

Melinda Christine Fox (our first granddaughter)
and Jon Peterson, the son of missionaries in Japan.
We sat in the church, listening to the low and
beautiful music of the organ, waiting for it to
burst out with "Here Comes the Bride," and thinking about Mindy. She was born about the same
time as our Robin—Robin who was born so retarded. At first Mindy seemed to be a perfectly normal
baby; she bubbled with smiles and sunshine and
the sight of her helped soothe my heart as poor
Robin struggled to survive. But Mindy developed
trouble when she tried to crawl, and the doctors
were consulted and they said that she had been
born with only one hip socket and would probably
have to drag one crippled leg the rest of her life.
I nearly broke when I heard it, but Mom took me
firmly by the shoulders and shook me and said,
"Get hold of yourself. Your son and his wife—Mindy's mother and father—need you now. Straighten
your face and go to them." I went. My going
proved to be the greatest therapy I had ever known.
When you're in trouble, go help someone with a
greater sorrow, and watch yours disappear!

They really didn't need *me*. Tom had a relaxed
trustful expression on his face, and Barbara said,
"The Lord knows about it and He will handle it,"
but that awful ache was still there. As it turned
out, God did take care of it. Mindy learned to
walk with no limp. And today she was about to
walk down the aisle!

I was jarred out of my reverie by the organ as it

burst into a wedding march that I had never heard before. It wasn't the old "Here Comes the Bride," but the old hymn "Thanks Be to Thee," in march time. The ushers led the five bridesmaids down to the little white picket fence around the altar, then my Mindy, walking straight and tall and confidently with a light on her face that brought tears to ours.

Jon and Mindy had arranged the whole service. That's a new one, to me, and I like it. I had been suspicious of it, in the past, for with some of our "hep" youngsters the ceremony had become almost a comedy. Not here! The service they had arranged began with all of us singing, "Sprit of God, descend upon my heart . . . Stoop to my weakness, mighty as Thou art, And make me love Thee as I ought to love." A Scripture passage was read by the pastor —Ephesians 5:22-33. A friend of Jon's sang "O Master, Let Me Walk With Thee." Christ was the unseen but invited guest at this wedding.

I saw firsthand the fruits of the labors of Christian parents in these two young people unashamedly confessing their love for Christ and each other. Each said, "I bring nothing to you but my love, my trust in and loyalty to our Lord; I can promise you nothing beyond that, but I will work together with you for a home in which Christ is the center." They exchanged rings; the Lord's Prayer was sung, and the bride and groom were presented with two roses.

The bride and groom then presented the roses

to the two mothers. The children embraced their parents and went up to three-pronged candelabra at the altar. One unlighted candle in the center puzzled me until I watched the lighting of the center candle and the snuffing out of the two outside ones—signifying that the work of the parents was finished, and that a new home had been created. The minister pronounced them man and wife.

The final touch: Jon and Mindy faced the congregation and thanked us all for coming and said it was their hope that everyone there might know Christ as they knew Him and find the same joy in serving Him. (Frankly, it was a two-handkerchief affair!)

Do you see what I am getting at when I say that the show goes on? Little Robin was gone, but here was Mindy establishing a home built on His love. One leaves, another comes on. He gives a life for every one He takes away. He closes one door and opens another. Blessed be the Name of the Lord.

Not long before this, I watched a TV show in my motel room, one of those "special human-interest spot shows," by a well-known newscaster. It was a series of flashbacks or shifts from one kind of wedding to another. There was the traditional wedding scene with the beautiful bride coming down the aisle on the arm of her father—then a quick shift to a so-called mod young couple who voiced their opinions of "the words said over you by some man, a piece of paper, and a golden ring on the finger, plus all the unnecessary expense."

They said it was all nonsense, that it was better simply to live together without all that, enjoy love (love?) as long as it lasted, and then "simply split."

The scene shifted to some mothers of my generation who voiced their opinions. One said, "Oh, let the kids do their thing, however they want it," but another said, "Well, I'm hopelessly old-fashioned; I'll take the church wedding, the minister, the piece of paper, the ring, the flowers—the works." Then a flashback to the mod couple, who admitted they were unmarried but living together. As the camera caught them, the girl had a pensive faraway look on her face—looking at what? an uncertain future with no pledge in love to bind them? Neither one of this couple looked exactly ecstatic. Frankly, it was to me a very anemic, pitiful performance.

Any dubious wonder I had felt during the long year of planning by Jon and Mindy was dispelled as the bridal couple went back up the aisle to the reception—a reception at which every face wore a smile of pure happiness. This wedding, I told myself, was the Lord's doing—and wonderful in my eyes. It was blessed of Him, as He had blessed the wedding in Cana of Galilee.

17

After All

I am very tired. The last week has been a rough one—just one thing after another. To begin with, I had to get Mom down to Texas. We drove out to the Los Angeles Airport, and in trying to negotiate one of the narrow roadways of that airport I did it: I put a dent in one of the car doors—a dent that you could drive a truck through. The next thing I did wrong was to walk into that man's occupied room. Nice start, Dale!

The next morning we boarded the plane—after being frisked. Mom doesn't like that frisking, but I don't mind it too much. They didn't find any guns or bombs, so they let us go aboard. We left an hour early, to have time enough to get the car parked and to get my crippled mother into the plane. *Then* we waited for an hour and a half to board! Mechanical difficulty. I fumed. I hate waiting for anything or anybody—for taxicabs, slow waiters in a dining room, traffic lights that don't turn from red to green quickly enough, people late for appointments, or long-winded speakers at banquets who precede me on the dais—and hotel elevators that stop at every floor before they stop at mine! I'm in a hurry. As Roy says, "Dale wants it done yesterday!"

Landing at Dallas, a porter pushed Mom along in a wheelchair until we reached some stairs and an elevator. She can't negotiate an escalator because of her bad hip, so we had to bounce her down the stairs one step at a time. It took us an hour and a half to collect our baggage. That always gets me uptight. I honestly think that sometimes it takes the air passenger longer to claim his baggage than it takes him to travel from New York to California. By now, Mom was pretty tired—and I was in a snit. But somehow we got her into the rented car outside—and the minute the car started, the *seat belts* started to scream. In dense traffic I tried both to drive and to disengage the belts, which were frozen tight. Mom's face was getting red and I knew her blood pressure was rising. I tried to control my tongue and my temper: "Mom, we'll just drive to the nearest filling station and get the pesky thing fixed. Don't worry." I pulled into a station and the attendant didn't seem to know one end of a seat belt from the other.

I called the car rental people and they said, "Tell the man to pull loose some wires under the hood." He did; he pulled the wrong wire and left us with no horn. We drove back, and they gave us another car. In this we arrived nearly two hours late at my sister-in-law's home. That night I managed a prayer: "Thank You, Lord. This has been a dilly of a day, but we thank You for bringing us here safely."

Later, of course—I laughed at it. *Why* had I been in such a hurry? If we'd arrived a whole day late, what difference would it have made? Sure, that long wait to board was tedious—but it's better to get the plane in working order than to take off and crash. Sure, the screaming seat belts were infuriating—but maybe their mechanisms were put together by impatient mechanics who rushed through their jobs when they should have been slow and accurate.

We're all in a hurry.

But why should we be? God was in no hurry when He made man and the universe. It took Him a long time to produce coal in the soil, but He had plenty of time. So have we—if we only knew it. *We are living—not on our time—but on His.* He will get us where He wants us to go, in *His* good time. He is infinitely patient with us blundering, hurry-up Christians. (It reminds me of the story I heard about a convict's ball game in the prison yard. One fellow was tearing around the bases furiously, trying to stretch a one-base hit into a triple, and an old man on the bench called out to him, "What's your hurry, man? You're serving twenty years!")

"Lord," says Matthew 18:26, "Lord, have patience with me . . . ." I pray that prayer often, since I have followed Jesus—the amazingly patient Jesus —through Palestine. I love the words of James in The Living Bible:

> Dear brothers, is your life full of difficulties and temptations? Then be happy, for when the way is rough, your patience has a chance to grow. So let is grow, and don't try to squirm out of your problems. For when your patience is in full bloom, then you will be ready for anything, strong in character, full and complete.
> James 1:2-4.

That came over loud and clear in the Holy Land. I found out there that when I let the Lord lead me I forgot all about being tired. Like so many of you, I have consumed enough aspirin and so-called relaxers to sink a ship, and peace didn't come. It came only when I gave myself to Him.

Patience is a great part of my faith. I don't have enough of it but I'm trying.

Speaking of my faith, Art Rush told me once that a number of people had asked him, "Is Dale really sincere in her beliefs and in her Christian faith?"

That question doesn't bother me; I expect it. You know, most people living under a constant spotlight, who boldly confess Jesus publicly, are suspect. It helps me to remember that our Lord was suspect by the religious and nonreligious alike in His day. He said that the servant was not above the master. Surely, we should not expect everybody to agree with us, or never to question our sincerity and motives. I can understand their wondering, for before I committed myself to Christ, lock, stock, and barrel, *I* was suspicious of what I thought were "religious fanatics," and I didn't want to be one of "those." But I knew well that some people would suspect me of being just that, sooner or later. You can't witness without meeting that question, and I believe in witnessing wherever I happen to be—let the chips fall where they may!

Not long ago I was on the set of a TV special which was being filmed in Las Vegas. (If witnesses are needed anywhere, it's in Las Vegas!) I was talking with another Christian in the cast about faith and religion, when a young star sitting near us turned to me and asked, "Are you a Jehovah's Witness?" It was a loaded question, and I took my time—patience, gall—answering it. I said, slowly, "I am just a Christian and a would-be follower of the Person of Jesus Christ." Apparently that satisfied her; she had no more questions.

As I write this, I am back in Las Vegas; I've just come in from a swim in the hotel pool. As I lay on the chaise lounge, drinking in the brilliant Nevada sunshine, I looked up into the deep incredible blue of the sky above me and thought of God's Creation. This relatively small terrestrial ball we call earth is but a fragment of God's illimitable imagination.

Who but He could do it? He has given us mortals so much and has asked so little in return—just our insignificant selves in appreciation of His Creation and His Son. The Person of Jesus Christ! How do we flaunt ourselves to the point of arrogance, thinking we can be the masters of our fate, ignoring the Creator and the One He gave in substitution for our failure to measure up to His Holiness?

What a presumption *that* is!

In the book *Nine O'Clock in the Morning*, Dennis J. Bennett tells of his shock when, on his very first night in the theological school residence hall, his next-door neighbor, a senior, and a very "ministerial," scholarly looking chap, came by to "cue him in."

> Of course, we no longer believe in the miracles of the Bible, the divinity of Jesus, or the virgin birth. Science has shown these to be impossible, also life after death, and other such things. We can no longer accept the supernatural. We must develop a natural, scientifically respectable religion that will be accepted by modern intellectuals.

Bennett goes on to reveal that one of the most respected professors, a tremendous scholar, began all of his classes with, "I want you to understand that I am an atheist!"

I don't know what led him to those conclusions, but I'm here to say that I have been led by Jesus

Christ into something more than a "respectable" faith. He never led me into atheism; I'd rather die than to live by such a code. The professor would probably call me a fanatic. I would much prefer to be a fanatic than a fool. I can *never* believe that an omnipotent and omniscient God created me and gave me such a glorious earth to live in and then turned me loose with the caution, "Of course, you can't believe in *Me*."

The professor can have his atheism; I'll take my Christ. He can "demythologize" God and the Bible if he wishes. To me God and His Son are no myth; they are as real to me as they were to those who met Christ and listened to Him and followed Him along the dusty roads of Judea and Galilee.

Madalyn O'Hare would call me a fanatic. I watched a television debate between Mrs. O'Hare and William Buckley. As I studied her face I was reminded of the words in the Second Psalm, "Why do the heathen rage and imagine a vain thing? (*see* v.1). When Mr. Buckley asked her if she believed in God she replied, in effect, "I am still searching." Well, that's encouraging, for it indicated that while she is searching she is still grudgingly aware that there just might be "something" beyond her intellectual grasp.

I'm not bitter. I feel as sorry for her as Senator Daniel Inouye felt when, as an American soldier, he went into a barbershop for a haircut and heard the bigoted barber say, "I don't cut hair for Japanese."

Mr. Inouye didn't get mad. He simply said, "I feel sorry for you," and left the shop.

I pity Mrs. O'Hare. In her adamant atheism, she is banging her head against a stone wall and doesn't know it. Saint John says that there is a "true Light which lighteth every man that cometh into the world" (1:9). That light was installed in our being by God our Creator. It is a searching light, searching out for us the truth of His Being. Trying to put out such a light is like trying to stamp out a forest fire with your feet—impossible!

Mrs. O'Hare thinks children in the fifth grade should study *comparative* religions. Just try that on your ten-year-old, and watch him become as confused as a Hottentot trying to read Greek! How can any child in the fifth grade understand comparative religions? Satan is a wily rascal, and I believe he has convinced her that it is "only fair" to allow the child to make up his own mind as to what he will accept or reject in religion before he is hardly out of his cradle! Did Mrs. O'Hare feed her infant son steak before he had teeth to chew it? Is it possible that these atheists figure that by throwing all the world's religions at the child at once, at a very early age, he will become so confused and frustrated that he will catalog all of it under "myth" and reject it as reality?

My Bible contains a letter written by the Apostle Paul to a young man named Timothy. The apostle warns his young friend to "continue . . . in the things which thou hast learned and hast been as-

sured of, knowing of whom thou hast learned them;
And that from a child thou hast known the holy
scriptures, which are able to make thee wise . . ."
(2 Timothy 3:14, 15). Paul was reminding Timothy that his mother, Eunice, and his grandmother,
Lois, had given him the basic truths of their faith
while he was a child. They had *not* loaded him
down with the teachings of the Greek mystery religions or Egyptian or Babylonian gods. They simply planted in their son and grandson the seeds of
faith in One who had come to give the world something better than all that, and cultivated it as it
grew and developed into maturity.

I wonder if Mrs. O'Hare finds any *good* thing in
all these contemporary religions which she could
not have already found in Christianity?

And does she not see that every civilization which
has rejected God and Christ has become decadent
and morally depraved and finally fallen into obliv-
ion? Does she want this for her grandchildren? If
she does, she doesn't know the meaning of the word
love; she does not know God and she is unaware of
His love.

I'm not trying to write a whole book on Madalyn
O'Hare. She is only one of a small minority who
are teaching the philosophy of anti-God and anti-
Christ. I believe that such teaching brings not freedom or anything else worthwhile—but disillusion-
ment and disaster. A psychologist said recently that
we parents have made a ghastly mistake in turning
a whole generation loose to do their thing—things

that poison both them and their country—with the result that we have produced "a generation of hard-boiled little monsters." I don't go for that word *monster;* I know our younger generation, taken as a whole, is not *that,* but I do sense the danger in this misguided permissiveness. I believe that such teaching is inspired of the devil—though, of course, the devil is probably a "myth" to Mrs. O'Hare. (I wonder if she would deny that a spirit or force of evil is at work in her world?)

I pray for her, and for her followers. She and they could be great forces for good. I believe that they "protest too much"; I can believe that she and they hear the footsteps of the Hound of Heaven pursuing them, and that they scream their defiance in fear of being apprehended by Him.

I have been so apprehended, and I am not ashamed of it. Say my faith is blind, call me anything you wish; you can never destroy my conviction that Jesus Christ is as Tennyson said, "Closer . . . than breathing, and nearer than hands and feet." I found Him so in Palestine—but I do not believe that we can or should *leave* Him in Palestine. We can find Him on any Main Street in the world.

I'll give her this much: I think she was right when she said, as I recall it, "If you Christians had been on the ball, I would not have been able to get prayer taken out of the public schools." We should take that remark seriously. She was right. Too many of us had left Him isolated in Palestine when she did that. And she will accomplish more if we don't get on the ball. We read our Bibles, go to church and to prayer groups, and get all fired up about following in His steps—and then we knuckle down at the first sign of ridicule from our peers. We keep silent while our Mrs. O'Hares sound off like steamboat whistles in ridicule of our church and our Lord. All evil men need to win is the silence of good men.

There are times when I have to stand in the face of open ridicule. That isn't easy—but did the Lord ever promise that it would be easy? He has promised us peace—the hard way. I am obligated to accept that when I accept Christ. And I believe I have an obligation to stand and be counted *in action* for Jesus Christ. These atheists disturb us—but maybe God uses them to disturb us into action. I believe we should disturb others—in reverse—in the direction of faith in Him. The English poet, Francis Thompson (who wrote *The Hound of Heaven*) said once, "thou canst not stir a flower without troubling a star." I love that. It says to me that every move we make influences (troubles) someone into either doubt or belief in the power and goodness of God.

In Palestine I saw the Mount of the Ascension—the Mount of Olives, where Jesus was taken out of their (the disciples') sight and returned to the Father. I remembered the words of the two men in white apparel who said to them, "Ye men of Galilee, why stand ye gazing up into heaven?" (*See*

Acts 1:9-11.) We have to do more than stare in
awe of Christ: *We have to go to work for Him.*
We need a *working* faith.

After all—that is all that matters to me.

Maybe I can sum this all up through the words
of an interview I had last spring. It went something
like this:

QUESTION

What is the most important thing in life for
you?

ANSWER

It is a working faith in God through Jesus Christ.

Once, with me, it was popularity in the entertainment business.

That was wrong. No matter what I did, it was
never enough.

My work then took me away from home too
much, and my children resented that.

But when I gave my life to Christ, He gave me a
new relationship with my husband and my
children.

I spent more time at home, making it a home in
which Christ was the heart.

I saw that faith was proved or ruined in family
relationships, in sharing and pulling together
in love.

When Christ was really given the ruling hand in
our family, we reached out from that home
base to world humanity. I feel there is nothing
more important than that reaching.

QUESTION

What do you consider the secret for becoming
stable and happy, and staying that way?

ANSWER

For me, the secret lies in understanding the
Scripture which says, "Thou wilt keep him in
perfect peace whose mind is stayed on thee."
And I find it in the hymn "Turn Your Eyes
Upon Jesus."
When I come head on against some drastic, unexpected change in my life, I accept it as just
another turn in the road. I do not know what
awaits me there, but I do know that whatever
awaits me around any corner, He is there to
help.
Since my joy no longer depends upon outward
circumstance, I know that He has established
my comings and my goings, and that He will
hold me fast and keep me stable.
I trust Him completely, knowing that He will
give me a measure of happiness in every
change, difficult or easy.

QUESTION

If you had to do it over again, would you
change anything in your life?

ANSWER

Yes. I would change a lot of things.
I would ask, earlier in my life, that Jesus Christ
take over as Master of my life.
I would be more obedient to my parents.

I would accept the fact that my parents knew better than I knew what was best for me.

I would not try to grow up too fast and take on adult problems before I was emotionally ready to cope with them.

I would be less anxious to do my thing and more anxious to do God's thing.

I would set myself to learn how to regulate my life better, instead of letting it run wild.

I would take more time to rest, to think, to pray.

I would not rush into marriage; I would ask God to guide me in the selection of my vocation, *and* my mate.

I would give heed to the words of Ecclesiastes 12:1:

Remember now thy Creator in the days of thy youth, while the evil days come not, nor the years draw nigh, when thou shalt say, I have no pleasure in them.

I would struggle early and late to draw nearer to God, to enjoy serving Him, to learn from Him.

I would strive for a better understanding of other people.

I would listen less to "what people say" about me or to me, and listen more to the still, small voice of God.

I would spend more time in the company of radiant, ongoing, happy, accomplishing people who walk with Him.

If I had it to do over again I would "let go and let God"—let Him have my life earlier, and more fully.

QUESTION

How do you advise young people to meet doubt and affliction and sorrow?

ANSWER

I try to make them see that God is a real help in time of *any* trouble; that "The Father knoweth what things ye have need of" (*see* Matthew 6:32)—and what things they *don't* need.

I tell them that He allows trouble and sorrow in our lives to draw us closer to Himself—and to appreciate the things that are pure joy when they come.

That just as parents have to correct their children, God has to correct His children—which includes all of us. He corrects us because He loves us and wants to teach us a better way.

That we can grow up into the people He wants us to be if we have the spirit and the courage to listen to Him.

That he makes us able to enjoy the good things more, and never just to take them for granted.

I advise them to analyze their sorrows and troubles, and find out how many of them are self-inflicted—like the trouble of the pneumonia you catch when you go out in the rain without your umbrella!

That they can't blame God for everything; so

much that is bad is the penalty we pay for *ignoring* God.

That when Jesus said, "I will not leave you comfortless . . ." (John 14:18), He meant that He would walk with them even in the valley of death, as He walks with them in the days of joy and prosperity.

That gems cannot be polished without friction, nor man be perfected without trials.

That if they list all their troubles and all their blessings they will soon run out of troubles.

That our difficulties should act as a tonic, driving us to greater efforts.

Thank God for difficulties!

QUESTION

How do you share your problems and everyday life with God?

ANSWER

I take life a day at a time.

I ask Him for guidance and strength just for that day.

I do not have yesterday, nor tomorrow—just today.

When I accept that day for what is in it, I will find miracles in it.

Jesus tells me, "Take therefore no thought [don't worry overmuch] for the morrow . . . Sufficient unto the day is the evil thereof" (Matthew 6:34). That has saved me oceans of anxiety.

In other words, I have enough to handle, with

God's help, on this one day. I am content to leave the rest in His hand, content that He will not leave me *comfortless*.

I thank God for the little things and the big things in every day: for life itself, for a world of beauty to live in, and for the beauty that outweighs the evil; for sunset and sunrise and another day to work for Him; for the love others have for me, and the love I have to share with them; for the gift of laughter; for the talents He has put in my hands; for His Presence all along the road.

I talk with Him and I walk with Him.

I pray without ceasing, audibly when I am alone, silently in the presence of others.

I seek His pardon immediately when I have gone out of line in thought, word, or deed, when I do those things I know I ought not to do and when I am not doing the things I know I should be doing.

I remind myself constantly of His promise, "Lo, I am with you *alway*."

Just the other day Roy called to me to look at a tree full of robins in our backyard. I looked and said, "Do not worry about what ye shall eat, or drink, or wear, or where you shall go or .... Those robins don't worry very much, do they?"

Roy said, "Do you know that you are worth more than many sparrows—or robins?"

Yes, I know. He has found me and He has led

me in Galilee and Judea and New York and California and everywhere I go. He has led me through many a dismal valley. He has led me to bright mountaintops where His Transfigured Being gleamed with light. That light has led me up to now, and it shall lead me tomorrow and tomorrow and tomorrow *and* tomorrow:

Where He leads me I will follow . . . .

I have come home from Palestine with the dust of His glory road on my feet and in my soul. I find the light of His countenance going before me on the common roads of home as I found it leading me there. And it lightens my journey through good and cloudy days, and gives me peace. And I live only to pray His peace upon all I meet along the way.